Praise for Douglas E. Noll's

DE-ESCALATE

When faced with someone's anger, we're inclined to react emotionally to the words hurled at us, responding with silence or more words hurled the other way. Neither tactic works to bring understanding or peace. Douglas Noll encourages us to ignore the words and work with the emotion to "de-escalate" the destructive passion in just a few minutes. This book is written so the reader can learn to work with understanding what's behind the anger by ignoring the words and focusing on the emotions and reflecting them back. I'll be recommending this book to clients with troublesome teens.

—**Dr. Georgina Cannon**, author of *The Third Circle Protocol*

The skills and techniques taught in this book and used by Douglas Noll and his colleague Laurel Kaufer have been instrumental in transforming the lives of hundreds of female inmates in California prisons. These skills have demonstrated that when utilized as they have been taught, they will help anyone de-escalate any argument, fight, or disagreement. I have observed the effects and benefits of using these skills within our programs. The end result was the ability to obtain resolution to many issues and bring about peace within the prisons in which they do this powerful work.

—**Velda Dobson-Davis**, retired chief deputy warden, California Department of Corrections and Rehabilitation

De-Escalate: How to Calm an Angry Person in 90 Seconds or Less is based, in part, on the pioneering work in listening skills by Robert Bolton, the recent advances in understanding neuroscience, and the work that Doug Noll and I have been doing in California prisons since 2010. This book explains the skills we teach and why they work and provides concrete examples for de-escalating highly emotional people. We have seen these skills tested over and over again in many workshops, and they work! Whether you are dealing with an upset child or a politically polarized family member, using these skills can keep you centered and in control and help you move through conflict productively.

—**Laurel G. Kaufer, Esq.**, cofounder of Prison of Peace

Doug Noll is one of the foremost thinkers, teachers, and practitioners of conflict resolution and mediation. We've taught together for more than a decade, and I'm still learning as I watch him transform skeptical mediators, judges, and law students into conflict de-escalators. He quickly trains hardboiled lawyers to affect label unsuspecting dinner waiters and Starbucks baristas to their amazement. They return the next day full of successful stories of developing deeper, empathic connections in seconds. In *De-Escalate*, Doug makes that research and practice-driven insight real through hopeful stories from the most hardened criminals. As usual, Doug spells it out so that you can de-escalate parents, supervisors, teachers, and other disputants immediately. Do yourself a favor—read the whole book. It will be another effective tool in resolving conflict.

—**Don Philbin**, mediator, adjunct professor, creator of
Picture It Settled, and curator of ADRtoolbox.com

De-Escalate: How to Calm an Angry Person in 90 Seconds or Less is a ground-breaking new book on truly effective listening. Doug Noll teaches us to ignore the words of an angry person and focus only on the emotions. Using techniques that have been shown by neuroscience to quiet the emotional centers of the brain, he can teach anyone how to manage strong, angry emotions while remaining calm. Anyone can benefit from this book and Noll's ideas. Strongly recommended.

—**Eric Galton**, professional mediator, Austin, TX

Doug Noll's latest book, *De-Escalate: How to Calm an Angry Person in 90 Seconds or Less*, is an extremely valuable addition to the conflict resolution and peacemaking literature. Doug builds on the current knowledge and literature in the field and adds to it by revealing skills developed through his years of experience as a mediator and peacemaker. His additions are grounded in neuroscience and refined in the Prison of Peace project. Just as he and his colleague Laurel Kaufer have trained hundreds of inmates in California prisons to be peacemakers and mediators, he now is making these valuable ideas and skills available to you, the reader. You can learn how to respond to any provocation calmly and compassionately. Follow his simple, elegant, counterintuitive steps and you will transform your life and the lives of those around you.

—**Ron Claassen, MDiv, DMin**, professor emeritus (peacemaking and conflict resolution) and coauthor of *Discipline That Restores* and *Making Things Right*

DE-ESCALATE

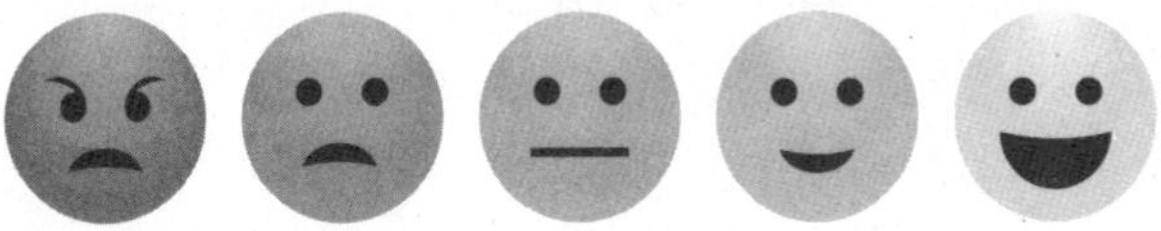

DE-ESCALATE

How to Calm
an **ANGRY** Person
in 90 Seconds or Less

Douglas E. Noll

ATRIA PAPERBACK
New York London Toronto Sydney New Delhi

BEYOND WORDS
Portland, Oregon

ATRIA
PAPERBACK

An Imprint of Simon & Schuster, Inc.
1230 Avenue of the Americas
New York, NY 10020

BEYOND WORDS
1750 S.W. Skyline Blvd., Suite 20
Portland, OR 97221-2543
503-531-8700 / 503-531-8773 fax
www.beyondword.com

Managing editor: Lindsay S. Easterbrooks-Brown
Editor: Emily Han
Copyeditor: Kristin Thiel
Design: Devon Smith
Composition: William H. Brunson Typography Services

First Atria Paperback/Beyond Words paperback edition September 2017

ATRIA PAPERBACK and colophon are trademarks of Simon & Schuster, Inc.
BEYOND WORDS PUBLISHING and colophon are registered trademarks of Beyond Words Publishing. Beyond Words is an imprint of Simon & Schuster, Inc.

For more information about special discounts for bulk purchases, please contact Simon & Schuster Special Sales at 1-866-506-1949 or business@simonandschuster.com.

The Simon & Schuster Speakers Bureau can bring authors to your live event. For more information or to book an event, contact the Simon & Schuster Speakers Bureau at 1-866-248-3049 or visit our website at www.simonspeakers.com.

Manufactured in the United States of America

20 19 18 17 16 15 14 13 12

Library of Congress Cataloging-in-Publication Data:
Names: Noll, Douglas, 1950- author.
    Title: De-escalate : how to calm an angry person in 90 seconds or less /
Douglas E. Noll, JD, MA.
        Description: Hillsboro, Oregon : Atria Books, 2017.
    Includes bibliographical references and index.
    Identifiers: LCCN 2017015967 (print) | LCCN 2017032606 (ebook)
        ISBN 9781501176258 (eBook) | ISBN 9781582706559 (paperback)
    Subjects: LCSH: Anger. | Interpersonal relations. | Interpersonal communication.
    Conflict management. | Psychology.
    BISAC: FAMILY & RELATIONSHIPS / Conflict Resolution.
        FAMILY & RELATIONSHIPS / Anger (see also SELF-HELP / Anger Management).
    Classification: LCC BF723.A4 (ebook) | LCC BF723.A4 N65 2017 (print)
        DDC 303.6/9—dc23
LC record available at https://lccn.loc.gov/2017015967

ISBN 978-1-58270-655-9
ISBN 978-1-5011-7625-8 (eBook)

The corporate mission of Beyond Words Publishing, Inc.: *Inspire to Integrity*

This book is dedicated to my wife, Aleya Dao.
I also dedicate this book to the inmates of Prison of Peace.
Each of you has been an inspiration to me.
I am so proud of you all.

CONTENTS

Foreword

Conflict. In today's world, it can feel as though we are being consumed by it. Discord exists in families, friendships, and the workplace. Turn on any news program or read any newspaper and you become witness to oppositional forces of governments, agencies, and individuals vying for power. That same news program will tell you about one human taking the life of another, domestic abuse, bullying, and a myriad of other unacceptable forms of aggression. Some form of conflict seems to permeate global society at every level, resulting in distrust and fear that ultimately erupts in an unproductive expression of anger.

What has brought us to the point where we accept disorder as a means of a resolution to a disagreement? What is conflict's cause, and how can we, as individuals and groups, alter the presumed consequence? Can we ever achieve peaceful conclusions to what may seem insurmountable disputes?

The answer to all of those questions can be found on the pages of *De-Escalate: How to Calm an Angry Person in 90 Seconds or Less*. This book provides us with an architectural blueprint needed to successfully navigate the smallest familial upset to the largest political conflict. And it all begins with emotional intelligence and the art of listening.

As co-founder of Prisons of Peace and through his work with the inmates of California's maximum-security prisons, Douglas E. Noll, JD, MA, has learned that the missing element of the equation is emotional intelligence, or "hearing" the emotions, not the words, of others. Mastering this process presents possibilities most of us only hope for, even though each of us has experienced some form of conflict.

Doug flawlessly describes the steps that can neutralize discord and explains that by learning to ignore the powerful emotional trigger of verbiage, we shield ourselves from turmoil and open the door to identifying the emotional experience of another person. With that knowledge, we can reflect and validate what they are feeling and access a path for communication. The result of utilizing these simple tools can and does de-escalate tension.

Those are just the cornerstones of the process, but they create a solid foundation that presents possibilities and actions that are affirmative for both parties. The value of the skills outlined in *De-Escalate* are incalculable. These tools can be successfully utilized in any strained setting. Their application can achieve goals that previously seemed hopeless and unreachable. What's more is that the implementation of Doug's techniques affords each of us the opportunity to learn more about another person as well as ourselves.

De-Escalate is a self-help book as much as one of intervention with others. Both aspects are imperative if we choose to live together in neutral harmony.

Douglas's de-escalation process requires retraining our mental and physical being to be more receptive on an emotional level. We must set aside ego and the immediate response to reciprocate a contentious environment with equal rancor. That process might initially feel like capitulation, but, in fact, it's the basis of a position of perceptive awareness. With that understanding, the real problems behind escalated tension can be identified, and the solution begins to unfold.

Imagine having the ability to sit down with your child and engaging in a productive discussion that reveals the core of what is bothering him or her. What would it be like to approach a derisive coworker in a way that facilitates calm resolution? Envision a process that could bring opposing civic leaders to a space where they might actually communicate. If politicians followed the path outlined in *De-Escalate*, we could all be the beneficiaries.

Doug developed this modality through years of experience as a trial attorney turned mediator turned peacemaker. The durability of his de-escalation process has proven itself time and time again. It affords anyone who reads this book the ability to enlist a method for more thorough understanding of and better communication with another human. In this day and age, *De-Escalate: How to Calm an Angry Person in 90 Seconds or Less* is a primer for everyone.

—**Brit Elders**, author and
CEO at ShirleyMacLaine.com

Introduction

Dear Ms. Kaufer,

My name is Susan Russo and I am an inmate at Valley State Prison for Women. I am writing in hope that you might consider doing a workshop on the proper techniques of mediation for our Networking Group. This group of women not only want to better themselves but also help others in general population. I feel a mediation workshop would not only benefit the inmates but also the staff. You would do the workshop with the ladies in the Networking Group, and then we will take what we have learned and teach it throughout general population.

I am hoping that you might consider this and that I will hear from you soon. Thank you for your time.

Respectfully,

Susan Russo, Valley State Prison for Women

Laurel Kaufer, my close friend and colleague, called me, read the letter she had just received from Susan, and asked, "What do you think?"

"I'm in," I said without hesitation. If we could teach prisoners to be peacemakers, we could prove once and for all that anyone could become a peacemaker and stop violence anywhere. If it could be accomplished in a violent, maximum-security prison, where would it not work?

Getting permission to begin the project was no easy task. Even though Laurel and I are both accomplished lawyers, it was our first experience with a prison bureaucracy. Finally, however, we received the go-ahead. We started with our first group of women inmates in April 2010.

At that time, Valley State Prison for Women had the reputation of being the largest, most violent women's prison in the world. The prison population was 3,480 in a facility designed to house 2,400 women. The fifteen women in our pilot group were all serving life or long-term prison sentences. They represented every walk of life, ethnicity, educational level, and socioeconomic background. They were tough, shut down, angry, and deeply wounded women. They were the forgotten untouchables of modern society. We had no idea whether our techniques would work with these hard cases, but these women wanted to end the fighting and arguing in their prison community and needed the skills to do it.

I cannot begin to describe the feeling of walking into a maximum-security prison on our first day. I am not easily intimidated, but walking through central control and hearing the multi-ton security door slide shut with a clang and loud click got my undivided attention—we were in the belly of the beast.

We were assigned to the D yard program office conference room. D yard was at least a quarter-mile walk through the outside main yard. The morning was a typical crisp and clear April day in Califor-nia's Central Valley. Laurel and I walked along silently, taking in the details of the prison environment: tall fences topped with razor-sharp wire, guard towers, large barren spaces with no vegetation—a bleak, depressing, and desolate place.

When we arrived at D program office, we immediately noticed the rectangular cages lining the wall and found out the cages were used to control angry inmates until the guards could deal with them. The yard sergeant showed us into the conference room. Dimly lit with fluorescent lighting and painted in institutional drab green, complete with concrete floor, this room was the definition of dingy. Half the chairs were broken and junked computers lay piled against the walls. It was cold and inhospitable. Laurel and I were used to teaching in bright graduate school classrooms or hotel conference centers. This was like nothing we'd ever experienced before.

Over the next fifteen minutes, our students made their way into the room. Black, white, Hispanic, young, middle-aged, old. All women. All long-termers or lifers. They were wearing prison blues with little or no makeup. A few wore dark glasses. Headwear ranged from baseball caps to do-rags.

I received some glares, suspicious looks, and skepticism; some of the women were meek and frightened. I could see the question in all their eyes: "What is this big, old, white guy lawyer doing here?"

And so it began.

In the fourth week of training, I realized that we had something powerful going on.

That day, we showed up at the prison early in the morning. I still had not gotten used to the heavy steel doors clanging shut behind me.

We began the quarter mile walk through D yard to the program offices and the shabby conference room that had become our classroom.

A tired fluorescent light flickered. One inmate, Sarah, had gotten there early. She was seated in a metal folding chair in a far corner. She was quietly sobbing. Laurel kneeled beside her. I stood at a discreet distance.

Laurel asked softly, "Sarah, what is going on?"

She was silent for a moment and then told us, "I've been in prison for years. I have a son who lives with my mother. I've written to him every week but haven't heard from him in three years. I only learn how he's doing through my mother.

"Two weeks ago, I decided to use the techniques you guys have been teaching me. I wrote him a different letter, using these new skills, describing how he must have been feeling all of these years. I basically affect labeled him in the letter, without ever talking about myself," she said, referencing one of the core listening skills we had taught a few weeks earlier.

Then she held up a piece of paper and a photograph. "Today, for the first time in three years, I received a letter from him. He's really angry with me but finally felt like I was listening to him. He's got a girlfriend, and he wants to come visit me," she said as she started to cry again. Obviously, they were tears of joy and happiness.

Laurel and I looked at each other. It dawned on us in that moment just how powerful these skills were turning out to be, how they were transforming these women's lives and the lives of their families. The power of listening and de-escalation skills had changed Sarah. That she could "listen" through a letter and get a response from her estranged son after years of silence was remarkable.

Since that day, we have witnessed hundreds of similar stories from inmates at both Valley State Prison and others. They have mediated disputes with parents, brothers, sisters, and children over the phone and during visits. One male inmate reconciled with his ex-wife after fifteen years simply by listening to her in a new way. Families, friends, and even fellow inmates noticed profound changes as our peacemakers gained mastery over de-escalation and deep, empathic listening through our program.

From Valley State Prison, we expanded into two more women's prisons and a men's prison. Eventually, we trained a cadre of inmates in each prison to take up the training of other prisoners themselves. In 2017, our Prison of Peace Project conducted workshops and classes for any prisoner wanting to learn how to de-escalate violent situations quickly; so far, over fifteen thousand inmates have been touched by six hundred peacemakers and mediators. With grant funding, we have expanded to a total of eleven men's and women's prisons. Some of these prisons have Prison of Peace because our trainers were transferred and immediately started teaching their new communities the practices of peace. In addition, one of our colleagues has started Prison of Peace in Athens, Greece. There are plans for Prison of Peace projects in Italy and France.

This ripple effect of peacemakers all started with a letter from one woman, Susan Russo.

The Prison of Peace Project has been one of the most profound experiences in my career. I've been deeply moved, over and over again, by inmates who have learned and applied deep, empathic listening, leadership, and problem-solving skills to reduce violence in their prison communities. Their dedication to learning, improving, and serving their communities is what motivated me to expand the principles of Prison of Peace as much as possible so that every human wanting to learn the skills of peace may do so.

It is my intention to teach you how to de-escalate any situation and person quickly and efficiently. You will learn to do so without losing control or composure. You will find a new competence and confidence in dealing with upset people in your family, at work, and in your community. You will be able to take insults, provocations, and disrespect from others without losing your cool. You will be able to stand in the presence of very strong emotions and say exactly the right thing in exactly the right way in exactly the right moment. In short, you will gain an immense amount of control over your emotional life. This will give you a power you never imagined possible.

As you learn and master these skills, you will experience five powerful transformations:

The *first transformation* will occur when you gain the insight that *we are emotional beings, not rational beings.* When you rid yourself of the idea that humans are rational, the actions and attitudes of those around you begin to make sense. You will be far less judgmental and critical while at the same time develop compassion and understanding.

The *second transformation* will occur when you learn about *emotional invalidation.* I call that the first deadly sin. It is pervasive and traumatizing. We are taught to invalidate the emotions of those around us as a way of managing our anxiety. When you become of aware of emotional invalidation, you will be empowered to stop it.

The *third transformation* will occur when you understand and can begin the practice of *affect labeling*—the skill to listen to other's emotions. The first time you successfully affect label an angry child or emotional partner, your life will be changed forever. You will experience the enormous power of deep, empathic listening.

The *fourth transformation* will occur sometime after you have been practicing affect labeling on others. At some point, you will find yourself affect labeling your own emotional experiences. You will find that you can *calm yourself down, become centered, and be less reactive no matter the provocation.*

The *fifth transformation* will occur when you experience *egolessness* while affect labeling. When you affect label another person, your ego will dissolve, experiencing your essence as it is truly is. This is a profoundly grounding state of being.

This book is written so that you can learn these skills and immediately apply them to whatever challenging situation you might face. When you have the confidence and ability to listen to and reflect the emotional experiences of those around you, you will experience these five transformations. And your relationships with your children, partner, family, and community will be easier, deeper, and more rewarding.

Arguments will no longer be necessary. Conflict will no longer be something to avoid or fear. As you grow and shift, those around you will do the same. You will be giving people in your life a precious gift of emotional competency, and by doing so, you will become both a mentor and a master peacemaker in a crucial time when we most need it.

Civility is at a premium in a society that is ruled by bombastic hyperbole, alternative facts (more on this in chapter 10), and outright aggression. In the supermarket line, at school, at the dinner table, in a corporate office, or in politics, the skills needed to deal with strong emotions, to solve problems, and to de-escalate angry people are sorely needed.

I have witnessed a handful of dedicated inmates change the culture of their prison from one of violence to one of peace. It only takes your effort to effect transformative change on all of those around you. As more and more people learn and practice the skills taught in this book, we will see a slow and marked increase in civility and peace. As political scientist and author Robert Axelrod's computer simulations proved in the 1980s, the doves can push out the hawks.

Axelrod wrote: "A world of 'meanies' can resist invasion by anyone using any other strategy—provided that the newcomers arrive one at a time. The problem, of course, is that a single newcomer in such a mean world has no one who will reciprocate any cooperation. If the newcomers arrive in small clusters, however, they will have a chance to get cooperation started."[1] Axelrod found that peace and cooperation were more efficient ways of negotiating conflict than aggression and violence. When introduced into a hostile environment of hawks, even a small group of doves eventually forced violence out.

We saw this effect in the prisons. As peacemakers and mediators were introduced in small groups to an environment where peace and cooperation were unknown, changes began to occur. There was less violence and less brutish behavior. A small group of our trained peacemakers and mediators changed the violent culture of their prison. I have no reason to believe that the same cannot occur in your life, family, and community if you and a few others are willing to learn these skills and use them in your everyday lives.

In short, mastering and practicing these de-escalation skills will:

- Minimize arguments
- Increase understanding and empathy
- Transform important relationships
- Allow people to be heard in a profoundly deep way
- Create a new space for civility

- Provide a mechanism for talking about hard issues between people with radically different beliefs

What to Expect

As we move through life, our priorities and tasks naturally change. This book has been structured to follow an organic, typical life arc with examples of real-life situations that I created for you to practice and master. While you might be tempted to jump around, you will learn the most by reading the chapters in order the first time through.

There are valuable and universal lessons, insights, and tools in each of the chapters, beyond the specific life theme and situation, which may not pertain to your life at this time. For example, you may not be a parent or grandparent and have little need to de-escalate an angry child or teenager; however, those two particular chapters still offer potent training, tips, and scenarios you can easily role-play. You will quickly recognize that learning to calm an upset teen can be useful in calming any emotionally upset person, whatever age and situation. So, my advice is: to master the de-escalation process, read all the chapters, and then feel free to go back to those that resonate in the current stage in your life arc.

Chapter 1 establishes the foundational skills behind the process of de-escalation, as well as the understanding that we are emotional beings, which will begin to help you listen in a new and powerful way. Chapter 2 puts into action affect labeling and how we can become empathic listeners. Learning how to respond to our children's meltdowns, anger, and frustration without emotionally invalidating a child's experience is one of the most useful and powerful points in this book—and an excellent entry point for practicing the de-escalation process.

My students always ask me, "Okay, I've calmed the other person down. What do I do next?" Well, chapter 3 answers that question by offering problem-solving skills we have found to be highly effective in Prison of Peace, specifically how to teach accountability and personal responsibility. Then, chapter 4 looks at the emotional terrain of teenagers. Teens have the task of forming new emotional attachments with peers, which often means ignoring or disrespecting the attachments with their parents and immediate family. This may be a frustrating time for parents, and knowing how to engage a teen is very useful indeed. This chapter also offers scenarios that deal with bullying and teach the effective use of peace circles to foster deep listening.

We then move to chapter 5, which introduces the skill of core messaging and also explains a powerful way to respond when you are insulted or disrespected. Chapter 6 takes us into the world where we form intimate and emotional attachments as couples, testing the feelings of commitment. It also delves into the complex emotions and listening skills needed in nurturing a healthy marriage as well as a relationship after divorce, in particular discussing what we know as the six needs of victims. Adult life also includes the complex terrain of our careers and professional relationships, which is another life theme I use in chapter 7. Finally, chapter 8 focuses on tools that you can use to de-escalate yourself, cultivating self-awareness and the transformative state of egolessness.

Chapters 9 and 10 are two specialized chapters. Chapter 9 takes us into the classroom. I have taught middle and high school teachers these de-escalation skills to great effect. In this chapter, I show how different classroom management looks when a teacher uses a firm and empathic response to misbehavior. It's an insightful chapter for all types of educators and for families as well. Chapter 10 takes us out into the world, addressing the serious problems that stem from the incivility and polarization we face in our ever-complex society. How do you listen to and de-escalate someone whose belief system is radically different from yours? And especially when that person is a family member, friend, or colleague?

As I tell my students, keep your mind open to these new ideas. Some of them will be counterintuitive and unusual. However novel they seem to you, remember that they have been developed and refined over a decade in very dark and highly emotional situations. As you will learn, there is hard science behind the skills. Trust the processes and practice them. You will find the changes happening sooner than you might expect.

1

The Secret Revealed

What I have learned is enormous. The listening skills alone have helped me a great deal. Just knowing there is an appropriate way to engage one another in conversation gives me clarity and confidence. They improve my relationships with friends, family, and strangers. I have learned to be quiet, wait my turn, and really listen to the person speaking to me. When I reflect back what they said, they actually feel listened to, and the genuine conversation surfaces.

Last week, I was called an idiot and I felt disrespected by an inmate from our pod. Instead of firing back or getting physical, I recognized my feelings and emotions, waited long enough to set them aside, and responded with a calm voice and attitude with resolution in mind. As soon as I reflected back that he is really pissed and that I am an idiot, he quickly apologized for snapping at me and explained that he felt disrespected when I did not listen to what he had been trying to tell me. I, then, apologized for not listening (I did not mean to disrespect him) and told him that I would accept his apology and feel a lot better about the whole thing.

Listening, reflecting, clarifying, and verifying works!

—**Bryce Markell**, Valley State Prison

Have you ever faced any of these people?

- An angry, upset person
- An emotionally unavailable partner
- A person with a different ideology or belief
- A bully
- A deeply annoyed boss
- A frustrated coworker
- An anxious, worried friend
- A sad, grieving family member
- An unhappy client or customer
- A silent, unresponsive child or teenager

How well did you handle this person? Did the problem get worse? Did you want to run, yell back, or stomp away? Did you get angry in return? Was there a huge argument or fight?

If you answered yes to any of these difficult situations, this book is for you. It will teach you how to calm an angry, upset person of any age in ninety seconds or less while remaining centered and calm. You will also learn how to calm yourself down quickly and efficiently.

The skills I will reveal to you have been tested in some of California's maximum-security prisons with inmates serving life sentences. These inmates have stopped violent fights, gang riots, arguments, and bullying using the skills in this book. Dozens of inmates have told me that if they had learned these skills ten, fifteen, or twenty years earlier, they would not be in prison today. It finally dawned on me that I should move outside prison walls and make the secrets available to everyone. Since then, I have taught these skills to middle and high school teachers, lawyers, judges, mediators, and graduate students. And now you.

Before we delve in, I want to first offer some background information on how I developed these de-escalation skills. When I first began working in the field of mediation, many of the skills taught to mediators and peacemakers were based on the experience of early practitioners; there was very little hard science and research on what really worked and why.

The field of neuroscience was fairly small in the late 1990s and early 2000s. Then it exploded as thousands of newly minted PhDs began their studies on the human brain, coinciding with my own serious study of human conflict. What I realized was that everything starts in the brain. Thus, I began to study the research literature, focusing on social psychology and cognitive neuroscience, to see what discoveries about brain function and process might be useful in bringing peace to the table. This culminated in the first published account of the neuropsychology of conflict, which was chapter 6 of my first book, *Peacemaking: Practicing at the Intersection of Law and Human Conflict*.[2]

Some of my early insights came from reading about the brain's fear reaction system, how neurotransmitters work, and in that regard, the critical importance of endorphins, dopamine, serotonin, oxytocin, and cortisol in modulating peaceful and aggressive human behaviors. I learned that humans are emotional beings with some capacity for reasoning and rationality. I learned that much of our behavior is automatic and that we don't have as much free will as we think we do. I learned about cognitive biases, distortions in decision-making, and the types of decision-making systems we have in our brains.

All of this changed the way I approached mediation, how I looked at others, and how I interacted with them in my work. I threw out any conventional wisdom about mediation and peacemaking that was not supported by science and began to explore ways to develop a practice and teaching based on applying the science to real-life situations. Knowledge is fine by itself, but I was driven to find better ways and tools to help people solve conflicts and problems—skills to de-escalate potentially violent people and situations as quickly as possible.

Years of research, experimentation, and determination led me to the work of UCLA social cognitive neuroscientists Matthew Lieberman and Marco Iacoboni, among many others. Their interest in how human brains process social information has provided me with deep insights into the practice of peacemaking. The de-escalation skills presented in this book are based, in part, on their discoveries, and the discoveries of others, creating practical, effective tools that any person can use to calm angry, emotional people.

We Are Emotional Beings

In this book, you will learn a new way to listen. Basically, you will learn how to listen for emotions and reflect those emotions to the speaker. This simple concept is both radical and countercultural, which is why it has not been widely taught before now.

In the history of Western philosophy, religion, and psychology, emotions have often been dismissed and judged as unreliable, dangerous, and even evil when compared to rational thought. We give much attention to the words people speak and almost no attention to their emotional experiences. If someone is experiencing an emotional moment, he or she may be called irrational, or worse.

The classical Greek philosopher Plato started the idea that emotions are irrational, and intellect or reasoning should take precedence over emotional reactivity. In *Phaedrus*, Plato described the human mind as a charioteer who commands two horses, one that is irrational and crazed and another that is noble and of good stock. The job of the charioteer is to control the horses to travel toward enlightenment and the truth. The takeaway, to put it simply, is: emotions are bad, rationality is good. It's a belief that has permeated Western thought for millennia—emotion gets in the way of reason.[3]

The early Christian church amplified this belief of reason over emotion through the philosophy of Neoplatonism. Augustine of Hippo (St. Augustine), the foremost theologian for the Church in the fifth century, incorporated Neoplatonism in his writings, and the result was that by mixing the Bible with ancient Greek philosophy, Christians began to struggle with emotion and reason. Neoplatonism found another adherent in one of the founding philosophers of the Enlightenment, René Descartes. Descartes is famous for his assertion: "I think, therefore I am" in his *Discourse on the Method*. Like those before him, Descartes rejected the importance of emotions, privileging reason over them.[4]

In modern terms, an analogy of this conflict is what I call the Spock Syndrome. Mr. Spock, as you probably know, was the science officer of the starship *Enterprise* from the popular *Star Trek* television show and film series. As the son of a Vulcan father and a human mother, he constantly wrestled with reason versus emotion, and this struggle created great dramatic effect in many episodes and movies. Generally, Spock would sink into emotional weakness, deal with his internal moral and ideological struggle, and finally deny his emotions. We would watch this morality play and feel relief as Spock came to his senses and once again was rational. The hidden message was that we all struggle between our emotional selves and rational selves. Only when the rational wins out by denying the emotional do we feel safe.

Gene Roddenberry, the genius creator of *Star Trek*, was well aware of the emotion-reason conflict in Western culture. He exploited this conflict skillfully. Spock epitomized pure reason in the Platonic ideal. The other characters in the show, such as Dr. McCoy, symbolized feelings and emotions. Scotty, the starship's engineer, was the technical expert in charge of the warp drive (which was in constant danger of blowing up, like emotions, and killing everyone on board). Of course, Captain James Kirk had to manage it all as the guy in charge.

The effects of the emotion-versus-reason conflict have persisted into modern culture. Culture teaches us from early on that emotions interfere with clear, logical, reality-based thinking. Unchecked, emotions distort perception and memory. Beyond that, emotions can get us into trouble if they are permitted to rule the brain. Emotions need to be restrained, moderated, and brought under control. In short, in contrast with rationality, emotions are treated as dangerous experiences to be avoided whenever possible.

Western culture, with its overemphasis on reasoning and rationality, has deprived us of the ability to manage emotions competently and develop our emotional intelligence. We assume that emotional skills will be taught as we grow up, yet other than learning basic social skills, there is no formal training in emotional competency. Some of us do learn to be emotionally intelligent, but many of us do not. The hard truth is that emotional competency is a skill that has to be taught and learned.

The cost of emotional incompetency can be measured by death and disease. If you live a life of arguments, fighting, and conflicts in your family and at work, you are killing yourself. Danish researchers have found that people who fight and argue suffer ten times more cancer, diabetes, and heart disease and are two to three times more likely to die than those who do not. The findings still held when chronic disease, depressive symptoms, age, sex, marital status, support from social relations, and social and economic positions were taken into account.

For that study, Rikki Lund and her colleagues at the University of Copenhagen collected data on nearly ten thousand men and women, ages thirty-six to fifty-two, who took part in the Danish Longitudinal Study on Work, Unemployment, and Health. Participants were asked about their everyday social relationships, particularly about who—among partners, children, other relatives, friends, and neighbors—made excess demands, prompted worries, or were a source of conflict, and how often these problems arose. Using data from the Danish Cause of Death Registry, the researchers tracked participants over a twelve-year span, from 2000 to the end of 2011.

The researchers found that stresses related to excess demands, conflicts, and arguments were linked to a 50–100 percent increased risk of death from any cause. Among all these stresses, arguing was the most harmful. Frequent arguments with partners, relatives, friends, or neighbors were associated with a doubling to tripling in the risk of death from any cause, compared with those who said these incidents were rare.[5]

In direct contradiction to Plato, the Neoplatonists, the early Christian Church, and Descartes, we now have found that human health and vitality is absolutely dependent on a healthy emotional environment. As the Danish study showed, chronic arguments, conflicts, and disputes do nothing except shorten lives. In addition, recent findings in neuroscience establish that reasoning and rationality depend on emotions. For example, in Pfister and Böhm's framework of emotional functions, emotions play four pivotal roles in rational decision-making:

- Providing information, through pleasure and displeasure
- Improving speed—for example, hunger, anger, and fear can all induce fast decisions
- Assessing relevance—for example, regret or disappointment can assist a decision maker in choices
- Enhancing commitment—for example, moral emotions such as guilt, shame, and love help decision makers commit to decisions affecting others rather than being drawn back toward pure self-interest[6]

Without emotions, we cannot reason. Without emotions, we cannot be human.

Let's try an experiment. If you have any kind device that has an audio advertisement that you can listen to, turn it on. It doesn't matter if it's a radio, smartphone, tablet, or desktop. It can be a video ad or purely audio. If you have a video ad, for this experiment, try not to watch the image. Only listen to the audio portion of the ad.

When you listen to the ad, ignore the words. That's right. Completely ignore the words being spoken. Instead, see if you can guess and name the emotions that are being communicated underneath the words. Name them silently as they come up. Guess them if you are not sure.

What were the emotions? How many different emotions were conveyed in a twenty- or thirty-second spot?

The first time I tried this, I listened to some dumb ad in a waiting room. I focused only on the emotions. In twenty seconds, I detected:

- Anxiety
- Fear
- Embarrassment
- Hope
- Excitement
- Relief

I was surprised at how many emotions were communicated in twenty seconds. As I thought about it, it made perfect sense. The ad was selling some product or another, and the speaker went through this range of emotions, from anxiety to relief. Of course, the relief was felt after the product solved the problem. To get there, the speaker had to experience all of these other emotions.

As the listener, I automatically experienced those emotions too, which was what the ad agency wanted me to experience. The intent was if I moved through a roller coaster of emotions in twenty seconds, along with the voice actor, I might associate hope, excitement, and relief with the product and buy it.

If you could identify even one emotion in the ad you listened to, you can de-escalate any angry person quickly and effectively. This will take some practice, but not too much. Ignoring words will also take some getting used to, because we normally only listen to the words but not the emotions. It's a different way of listening and responding that turns out to be a powerful tool, a tool that has changed many lives in the Prison of Peace Project and a tool that I use daily in my professional mediation practice and personal life. As soon as you learn it, you will use it daily and will discover how effective it is in changing the course of your life.

The Secret to De-Escalating

I intend this book to be the beginning of a new way of being, where our ability to work with emotions is equal to or greater than our ability to reason, engage in rational thinking, or problem-solve. By developing our emotional intelligence, we learn a crucial secret about de-escalating any angry situation or person in seconds. That secret is to do two simple things:

1. Ignore the words.
2. Guess at and reflect back the emotions.

As simple as this reads, it does take a mental adjustment to overcome the cultural aversion to emotions. And, like any new skill, it takes some practice. Not a lot, mind you, but some. Before we practice and master this process, let's take a moment to understand some important terms that I will be using. These terms are:

- Affect Labeling
- Emotions: Affect and Feelings
- Emotional Categorization
- Emotional Granularization
- Alexithymia

Affect Labeling

Affect labeling is the process of listening to another person's emotional experience and reflecting back those emotions in short, simple "You" statements. A typical affect label would be: "You are angry." I intentionally use the term *affect labeling* (not *effect*) because it most accurately describes the process of listening to and reflecting another person's emotions. It is a well-known term in the technical literature, and it should be more broadly used in our everyday conversations to describe the way we go about calming people down.

Unlike with other forms of reflective listening, when you wish to calm someone down, you must ignore the words and pay attention to the emotions. This is counterintuitive to many people. We are trained to pay attention to words from the time we are born. Words communicate a lot of useful information. We are conditioned to speak, read, and listen to words. Because this skill is deeply engrained in us, we do not learn how to listen for emotions. Yes, we can recognize when someone is upset or angry, but we are not really listening to their emotions in a deep way.

That's why the secret to de-escalating an emotional person in less than ninety seconds is learning how to ignore the words and pay attention only to the emotions. When you have mastered this, you can calm most people down quickly and easily. There are, of course, situations where calming someone will not work and may not even be appropriate. However, those situations are generally rare in our everyday lives. We are concerned with the more common types of arguments, anger, frustration, and annoyance. These emotions, if not resolved, may lead to fights or, worse, violence.

Emotions: Affect and Feeling

Emotion is a complex set of physical, cognitive, and mental attributes that we give to certain experiences. The physical part of emotion is composed of two parts: *affect* and *feeling*.

Affect is the word used to describe the physiological changes that occur within our brains in response to a memory or outside event. Imagine that you are on a desert trail and you see a coiled rattlesnake. Instantaneously, unconscious systems in your brain activate as neurons fire and neurochemicals are released in response to this sudden danger. This brain activity, when it arises in the emotional centers of the brain, is called affect. Affect is one of the biological foundations of emotion.

Although there is some disagreement within science circles about the number of affects we are endowed with, I prefer psychologist Silvan Tomkins's nine affects model. In his model, affect is categorized as positive, neutral, or negative. The following illustration lists these nine affects:[7]

Postive Affect	Neutral Affect	Negative Affect
		Fear-Terror
Interest-Excitement		Distress-Anguish
	Surprise-Startle	Anger-Rage
		Disgust
Enjoyment-Joy		Dissmell
		Shame-Humiliation

When I talk about these nine affects, I'm going to focus on six and rephrase a couple. For example, I leave out *Dissmell* and add *Grief-Shame-Humiliation* and *Abandonment/Unloved*. Dissmell was identified by Silvan Tomkins as a basic affect. It is the automatic response we have when we smell something rotten, like rotten milk or fresh feces or decaying organic matter. Dissmell is triggered when the smell stimulus reaches the brain, the head draws back and away, and the upper lip wrinkles. However, it is not a word that we use to describe emotions, and to simplify things, we can drop it from our short list.

Experience has taught me that underneath anger and fear, people are often experiencing deep unresolved grief. Many people also experience abandonment and feel deeply unloved. These are added to the list because they arise often.

Each of these affects is associated with systems within the brain that respond to environmental cues and memories. For example, the affect of fear is deeply associated with a part of the brain called the amygdala. Disgust seems to originate in the insula and so forth. Some brain systems are well-known; others are not yet fully understood. The good news is that we do not have to be neuroscientists to put this knowledge to use. The important takeaway is that these brain systems react outside of our consciousness in response to what's in our immediate environment.

The other physical aspect of emotion is what we commonly call feeling. When I get frustrated, for example, my face flushes deep red. My red face is caused by blood rushing into my capillaries. I feel hot and flushed. I have learned that this feeling is associated with something around me that I have labeled as frustrating.

So, to recap, emotion has two physical attributes:

1. Affect: What is happening in the brain
2. Feeling: What is happening in the body

Emotional Categorization

Emotion also has a mental, or cognitive, aspect. For us to be able to make sense of what is arousing us, we have to create a mental system of emotional categories. From life experience, we learn how to take the affects and feelings of anger and categorize them into the emotion of anger. This mental process is called *emotional categorization*. Without going too deep, this requires us to develop an appraisal process. Basically, our brain and body are aroused by something, we appraise, we find a category, and we label. Emotional categorization has turned out to be an important piece of human development. It is learned from experience and is very much influenced, if not defined, by our surrounding culture. This part of emotion is, therefore, socially based. One of the most potent skills you can teach your children is how to categorize the emotions they are experiencing in the moment. As they learn how to organize and categorize their emotions, they develop the capacity for empathy and communication.

Emotional Granularization

Following emotional categorization is the idea of *emotional granularity*. Emotional granularity describes the detail with which we can label an emotional experience. People differ in their degree of emotional granularity: low granularity means that Joe will experience the affect of anger, for example, but not be able to communicate his experience. He will just want to go out and hit something because he has no way to express to himself or others what is going on inside him.

Medium granularity means that Mary will experience the affect of anger and will be able to categorize it as anger. She can communicate in a rough way that she is angry. High granularity means that Peter will experience the affect of anger, categorize it as the emotion of anger, and further categorize it as intense annoyance.

People with high degrees of emotional granularity tend to have higher emotional intelligence, have better self-control, and be able to make better choices under the fire of emotion. People with lesser degrees of emotional granularity have less emotional intelligence, less self-control, and a harder time making good choices when upset. Here is an illustration showing the degrees of emotional granularity:

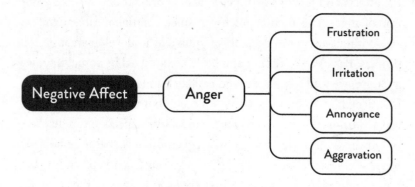

Alexithymia

The last term is *alexithymia*. It's a big word, but it's an important idea. People who experience alexithymia are unable to express their emotions with any degree of precision or depth. They lack emotional granularity. As a result, they tend to be reactive when their emotions are kicking. They default to automatic and unconscious behavioral programs. We have all seen people with hair-trigger tempers. They typically have very little emotional granularity and react instantly and unthinkingly to provocation.

In one study of domestic violence offenders, the men rarely reported emotion; rather, they described the acting out or release of affect through aggression and violence toward women. One man, age twenty-one, described a conflict in which he used violence to convey his emotional response. Shortly after he separated from his girlfriend, he ran into her at a club and later went home with her:

> She demanded for me to tell her how I felt, and I told her how I felt, and she said, 'Well that's not good enough.' And I kept telling her,

you know, I just want to be left alone. So she kept going on and on, because she had found a button to push. And so I kicked her off the couch and said, *'This is how I feel!'* And then I hit her. And that was that.[8]

He was unable to express himself emotionally, and his alexithymia was a direct source of conflict in his relationship; therefore, he used physical aggression as a way of expressing his affect of anger and frustration. This is a classic example of violence caused by low emotional granularity.

The important takeaway is that categorizing a core affect into an emotion turns it into a discrete experience. It allows what is going on in our brain and body to pop out in our awareness and take on meaning. Without emotional categorization, we cannot understand what we are experiencing, we cannot figure out what might be causing the experience, and we cannot communicate our experience to others. Emotional categorization is crucial. Until we can get our heads around what we are experiencing, our brains simply cannot think.

And that gets us to the core principle of affect labeling: *when we affect label, we are providing the upset person with the emotional categorization and granularity that they cannot, at that moment, provide for themselves.* We are, in essence, loaning out our prefrontal cortex to help another. By affect labeling, we help an upset person grasp and label her affective and somatic experience and concretize it into consciousness. Once the emotion becomes labeled in awareness, the speaker can work with it. As a result, she calms down. It is amazing to experience.

Three Essential Steps

As you start to affect label others, you will want to go slowly. Pick safe, low-risk situations during which to practice. As you gain confidence, you may take on more challenging situations. To begin this practice, we start with the basics and expand. Here are the three essential steps to affect labeling:

1. Ignore the words being spoken.
2. Guess at the emotions.
3. Reflect the emotions with direct, declarative statements. (For example, "You are angry, frustrated, and sad.")

Let's go through each of these steps, one at a time.

Step One: Ignore the Words

This seems so counterintuitive to what we know. After all, words are symbols that express and communicate meaning. Why do we ignore them?

First, if you are listening to the words, you cannot listen for the emotions. Our brains have the capacity to focus on one task at a time. So, when we consciously choose to ignore the words, we are freeing up our brain processing power to focus on the emotions.

Second, angry people say nasty, mean things. If you listen to the words, you are likely to become emotionally triggered. You can easily be sucked into the conflict whirlpool. By ignoring the words and focusing on the emotions, you are insulating yourself from the upset. The words lose their bite because you don't have time to think about the insult.

For practice, do the listening experiment at the beginning of the chapter. Listen to a television or radio or internet ad, ignoring the words and guessing at the emotions. Practice this until you can consciously turn off the words. You will master this very easily once you try it.

Step Two: Guess at the Speaker's Emotional Experience

How do you know what emotions another person is experiencing? First, don't think about it. This part comes naturally because we are hardwired to be empathic. All we have to do is pay attention. If we intentionally focus on the emotional experience of the other person, there are parts of our brain that will recognize, identify, and label the emotions for us effortlessly. This is not something we have to concentrate on; it will happen naturally.

To make it even easier, if we limit our list of emotions to the nine affects, we will cover 100 percent of all emotional experiences. Since we are interested in de-escalation, we really only have to remember six fundamental affects. In the usual order of presentation, they are:

- Anger
- Fear
- Anxiety
- Disgust
- Grief-Shame-Humiliation
- Abandonment/Unloved

To practice focusing on an emotional experience, watch television or listen to a radio ad again. Actors are good at portraying emotions. How good are they? Ignore the words, and using the list, label the emotions as they come up. You will observe that emotions change quickly. Keep with the basic list and label every emotion that comes up. You will find that you do not have to think much about this. If you let yourself go, the emotions will come to you automatically.

Since we cannot be inside of someone else's head, we really are guessing at their emotional experience. However, humans have a limited repertoire of emotions. If you stick with the basic list, you will almost always be right. The other good thing is that there is no penalty for guessing wrong. Usually, if you label the wrong emotion, the speaker will correct you, saying, "No, I'm not angry. I am frustrated!" In that case, you simply repeat the affect label by saying, "Oh, you are frustrated." I have never heard of or experienced someone becoming upset because the wrong emotion was labeled. People are so grateful that you are trying to really listen to them that they don't criticize your mistakes.

Step Three: Reflect Back the Emotions Using Declarative "You" Statements

This is just as simple as it seems. The most effective statement is the short, declarative "You" statement. For example:

"You are angry."
"You are frustrated."
"You are anxious."

Decades ago, people were taught to use an "I" statement when engaging in reflective listening. For example, "What I think you are feeling is anger." This does not work well in affect labeling. When you affect label, you must be focused completely on the speaker. There is no room for your ego. Your "I" must remain parked outside, and the easiest way to keep your ego in check is to use "You" statements.

My students sometimes protest that using a "You" statement seems presumptuous or rude. The objection is based on the student's fear of looking stupid, being wrong, or appearing incompetent. Ego is getting in the way. The best way to learn this is to test it yourself.

Find a willing friend. Tell him that you want to experiment with an idea you have been studying. Ask your friend to tell a short story about something that happened in the past day or so. Try affect labeling using "I" statements; switch and use "You" statements. Then ask your friend what the experience was like. Most of the time, people will report that they felt deeply listened to when "You" statements were used and not listened to at all when "I" statements were used. Check it out for yourself. Try this on several different friends to get a good sense of the power of "You" statements.

As you affect label an angry or upset person, watch carefully for three things:

First, listen for some kind of verbal response. Usually this will be an "Uh-huh," or something like it. Oftentimes, you will hear a "Yeah!" with a strong emphasis. This happens when you have connected with the speaker. The speaker is unconsciously affirming that you understand.

Second, watch for dropping shoulders. When people are angry, they tense their shoulders and raise them. When they calm down, they relax their shoulders so that the shoulders drop. This is another unconscious indication of de-escalation.

Finally, watch for a sigh, exhalation, or other sign of relaxation. In addition to the verbal response and the dropping shoulders, you will often witness such an unconscious indication that the person is calming down.

What It Looks Like

Here is an example of basic affect labeling between two friends:

Speaker (S): "My husband never listens to me. He just comes home and turns on the television."

Listener (L): "You are frustrated and feel disrespected."

S: "Yeah! And anytime I ask him how he is feeling, he completely shuts down."

L: "You are frustrated and sad because he will not connect with you."

S: "It can be so lonely at times. It's like we are living in two universes."

L: "You are lonely and sad, and you feel unloved."

S: "Yeah, that's it exactly. Thanks for listening to me." Head nods, shoulders drop, and she sighs in relaxation.

L: "You're welcome. Anytime."

It is as simple as it looks.

In the beginning, you may feel uncomfortable with the connection you are creating. You may also feel like you are intruding on the speaker's private space or being presumptuous or impertinent. These are your feelings and have nothing to do with the speaker, and being afraid of how you look will distract your attention away from the real focus: the speaker. That fear will eventually go away as you practice and witness the power of the de-escalate process.

Chapter Summary

In this chapter, we learned about:

- How we are emotional beings, and how by developing our emotional intelligence, we can de-escalate an angry situation or person
- A new way to listen: Ignore the words and listen for the emotions underneath
- Affect Labeling: The skill of reflecting a speaker's emotional experience back to them
- Emotions: A complex physical and mental construct describing affect and feelings

⊚ Affect: The result of the activation of brain systems associated with basic emotions
⊚ Feelings: The physical result of the activation of brain systems associated with basic emotions

• Emotional Categorization: The learned skill of organizing and categorizing affect and feelings into discrete mental constructs
• Emotional Granularity: The learned skill of putting very precise meanings to degrees of emotions
• Alexithymia: The inability to describe one's emotional experience

We have also been introduced to the three essential steps of affect labeling:

⊚ Ignore the words being spoken.
⊚ Guess the speaker's emotional experience.
⊚ Reflect back the emotion and use direct, declarative "You" statements.

2

Affect Labeling in Action

I've been using these skills with my ten-year-old son, not as a means of de-escalation, but to avoid conflict altogether. Conversations that used to become arguments no longer do. In the past, he would tell me a story in which he was always the victim (in his mind), and I would immediately see what his part was and gently try to share it with him, in hopes he'd learn from the experience. His response was to shut down and get defensive. Now, when he tells me the story, I speak to the emotions instead. He feels heard and understood and has been so much more open to feedback. It has had such an amazing impact on our communication, which makes for an even better relationship.

—**Dottie Sinor**

De-escalating Upset Children

Affect labeling requires practice. In the beginning, find safe situations where mistakes will not haunt you. If you have children, or work or care for them, they can easily provide you with opportunities every day.

We will improve affect labeling by considering how to de-escalate upset children from age two to eleven. As kids approach puberty, their sophistication and cynicism increases, requiring a higher level of skill. For now, if you can work with younger children, this will give you a good sense of how well de-escalation works. If you don't currently have these opportunities, this chapter is still valuable in showing you affect labeling in action, providing scenarios that are useful for other areas in your life. You can visualize and role-play these examples as a means to practice your affect labeling skill. Plus, you never know when you might find yourself unexpectedly confronted with an upset child.

In this chapter and subsequent ones, I've created a number of scenarios that capture common aggravating and escalating behaviors. These example scenarios provide you with ideas about how to approach angry conversations and conflict situations from a different perspective, and see how versatile affect labeling can be as an effective tool. When it comes to de-escalating children, less is more. You do not need much to calm them down. Let's start.

Sibling Rivalry

One age-old conflict is sibling fighting. The classic conflict occurs when the older sibling hits a younger one, starting a cascade of predictable events. The younger child screams bloody murder, running to you, exaggerating the strike, and blaming the older child.

"Mommy, Caitlyn hit me, and it hurt."

This all occurred in the other room, so you could not bear witness to what really happened. In all likelihood, Caitlyn did smack

Johnnie, based on past experience. Here's one way to de-escalate the situation and get the children to calm down.

> **You (Y):** "Why did you hit your little brother?"
> **Caitlyn (C):** "Because he was bugging me."
> **Y:** "You were annoyed and frustrated."
> **C:** "He wouldn't quit bothering me."
> **Y:** "You were angry and annoyed."
> **C:** "Yeah. I wanted to be left alone."
> **Y:** "You feel disrespected and not listened to."
> **C:** "Yeah."

There are some things to observe here. You start with a question to get some kind of response. Caitlyn answers not by denying that she hit Johnnie but by excusing her behavior as a retaliation against his instigation of the fight.

Your response is to not reason with or admonish Caitlyn. All you want to do is reflect what you guess she might be feeling right now. Your first affect label elicits another justification and excuse. Your response is to stay with what Caitlyn is probably feeling. It can be repetitious, and that is okay. Sometimes, you will repeat an emotion three or four times before it finally catches.

In the third response, Caitlyn finally talks a little about her need and how she felt violated. Your response acknowledges how Caitlyn probably felt: her little brother disrespected her and did not listen to her. This was the key, and Caitlyn responds with a "Yeah," a head nod, and visible relaxation. You are done with the de-escalation. You can now engage in some problem-solving, counseling, or corrective action (I will share more on problem-solving in chapter 3).

This exchange might take less than fifteen seconds, far less time than trying to argue with Caitlyn and listen to her become angrier and angrier. Caitlyn may be completely in the wrong. She might even be lying about what happened. However, until you get her calmed down, you don't have a hope of sorting out the situation.

Kids don't hit their siblings without some reason. We can surmise that Caitlyn had some affect and feeling going on inside of her. She was incapable of expressing what she was feeling to Johnnie in a way that he could understand. To Caitlyn's untrained brain, lashing out was the only thing she could do to resolve her own frustration.

By creating the space to affect label Caitlyn, you provided her with a valuable service and a lesson. You helped her understand what she experienced, categorized it into an emotion, and granulated it into specific words. What a precious gift. Repeated over and over during her childhood, this gift will pay off in huge dividends for Caitlyn.

You calmed Caitlyn down pretty quickly. What about Johnnie? Here's how that might go:

> **You (Y):** "Why did your sister hit you?"
> **Johnnie (J):** "I don't know. She doesn't like me."
> **Y:** "You felt ignored by your sister."
> **J:** "She never pays any attention to me."
> **Y:** "You don't feel loved by your sister."
> **J:** "She always treats me like a little kid."
> **Y:** "You feel disrespected. You are sad that your sister treats you like a little kid."
> **J:** "Yeah."

Again, you start with an open-ended question, which Johnnie responds to. At first, he says he doesn't know why and then adds a possible reason. Johnnie is trying to explain something that he may not understand too well himself. You reflect how he might be feeling: ignored. Johnnie responds by agreeing with your label and providing himself (and you) with an explanation of why he feels this way. This is great progress. You don't need to comment on his reasoning. Instead, you stick to his emotional experience and label again. Johnnie searches for another explanation and comes up with it. You reflect back his emotions again and get the "Yeah."

Johnnie may or may not have provoked Caitlyn. What affect labeling provided was some deeper information about what Johnnie was feeling. You and Johnnie learned that Johnnie's frustration stemmed from being treated like a little kid. Like Caitlyn, Johnnie did not have the cognitive capacity to associate affect with emotions, and he may have reacted to his frustration by provoking Caitlyn. It's classic conflict behavior. What's amazing is how we carry these conflict patterns into adulthood. As a mediator in complex business conflicts, I see the same patterns over and over again. If you are observant, you will see the same patterns emerge in our polarized social environment.

Emotional Shutdown

Another common situation is emotional shutdown. Imagine you are picking your child up from school. She gets into the seat beside you. You are happy to see her and want to connect. You use a conventional starter and ask, "Evelyn, how was school today?"

Evelyn looks out the window away from you and barely registers an answer. Your hope to engage your child is dashed yet again. Here's another way you might consider approaching Evelyn:

You (Y): "How was school today?"
Evelyn (E): "I don't know. It was okay, I guess."
Y: "You were frustrated because it was boring."
E: "It wasn't boring. I just don't like Mrs. Jones."
Y: "You were unhappy with Mrs. Jones."
E: "Yeah. She called on me and made fun of my answer."
Y: "You felt disrespected and embarrassed."
E: "Yeah. A couple of kids made fun of me at recess."

Y: "You were sad and a little lonely."

E: "Yeah."

You start with the opener. Evelyn responds with a noncommittal, nonengaged answer. You have to guess at what she is feeling, so you take a stab with boredom. You are wrong, and Evelyn corrects you. Notice that she does not criticize you or call you out for being wrong. She simply corrects you. This is how it happens 95 percent of the time. You follow with unhappiness and strike gold. Evelyn agrees with your label and gives you more information. Now you can sense that in class Evelyn felt disrespected and embarrassed. Evelyn opens up a little more about what happened at recess. You label what she is feeling—sad and lonely—and she relaxes.

You have to be patient, caring, and nonjudgmental for this to work. If you rush it or try to fix things before your child has sorted out the problem, your child will feel ignored and, worse, unloved. Affect labeling is powerful as long as you keep your needs in check and focus completely on your child. Anything less than that will cause failure.

The good news is that your intense focus only has to last about thirty seconds or so. This is a fast process once you have it figured out.

Lying, Denial, and Disobedience

Another common misbehavior is blatant lying or denial. William just hit his sister in your presence. Here's how you might consider approaching his blatant denial:

You (Y): "Why did you hit your little sister?"

William (W): "I didn't hit my sister!"

Y: "You are afraid of being punished."

W: "No, I'm not."

Y: "You don't feel listened to or heard."

W: "Yeah. No one cares about how I feel."
Y: "You feel lonely and unloved."
W: "Yeah."

The typical parental response is to challenge William. William digs in and vehemently denies he did anything wrong. You both know the truth, but now the argument is turning into a power struggle over face-saving. Your win will result in William's punishment, which will teach him little. Guessing at William's real emotions takes some imagination, but not much. If you open yourself up to sensing what he is experiencing inside, you will guess correctly.

Here's another common situation: disobedience.

You (Y): "Eat your beans."
Megan (M): "No! I don't like them."
Y: "You are annoyed and frustrated."
M: "I don't like them. I'm not going to eat them."
Y: "You don't like being told what to do. You are sad that no one loves you."
M: "Yeah. No one pays any attention to me."
Y: "You feel alone and unloved."
M: "Yeah."

In the previous three examples, reflecting that the child felt alone and unloved did the trick. Most children feel alone and unloved at times, and their reaction to the pain is to act out, which causes conflict. Your job as a parent is to recognize the source and acknowledge it, whether or not you believe the feelings—of being alone or unloved—are true. The point is to help label and validate the emotions the child is experiencing in that moment. That's the doorway to moving past the conflict and restoring calm. (I say more about emotional invalidation soon.)

Becoming an Empathic Listener

Affect labeling is a powerful form of empathic listening. Empathy is the ability to experience the emotional state of another human being, so becoming an empathic listener is the process of learning how to read and understand the "emotional data field" of another.

Some years ago, I was working with a group of high-level consultants on their leadership skills. Many of them were engineers, who tend to be critical thinkers who like hard data. I quickly realized that I had to come up with a concept around emotions that would engage them. It occurred to me that emotions are a form of data. The data is fleeting and sometimes ambiguous, but it is still data. In the middle of a workshop, I coined the term *emotional data field*, and the consultants immediately got it. They took up the challenge of reading the emotions of others as a form of data that could be collected, interpreted, and acted upon, thereby becoming excellent empathic listeners.

When we begin to think of emotions as a form of data, we can understand better what experiences others are having in the moment. The typology, quality, intensity, and duration of emotional experience are bits of information we can access quickly and intuitively if we pay attention. That is the essence of becoming an empathic listener.

We humans do not experience emotions in isolation. My experience has been that emotions show up in layers. Each layer has a depth and quality about it. Part of the problem people have with their emotional experience is that a loud layer will mask a deeper, more profound layer. They can scream and yell in anger but receive no relief because the underlying layer, still hidden, is active. This is especially true for children who have not yet developed adult tools for managing strong emotions.

As an empathic listener, you may wish to affect label through the emotional layers until your children acknowledge what they are experiencing. From the previous scenarios, I track the emotional layers like this:

Layer 1: Anger, rage, frustration
Layer 2: Disrespect, betrayal, unfair (not really an emotion, but it works)
Layer 3: Anxiety, fear, afraid, scared
Layer 4: Grief, sadness
Layer 5: Abandoned, unloved, unworthy

Start with the layer that seems to be presenting first. Usually in escalated situations it's anger or frustration. After each response, try a different layer. In the beginning, you have to trust your instincts about what emotions might be there. Using the typology above, listen and guess at what might be below the surface. Remember that emotions are a form of data in a field. Sense what your child is processing and go with that layer. Sometimes you have to circle back to an earlier layer before going deeper. Be careful about going too deep too fast in the beginning. Dip your toes in your child's emotional waters before you leap in headfirst. You will see how the layers work as you gain practice.

Conflicts over Technology

One of the great parental challenges of our culture is kids' obsession with technology, such as television, cell phones, texting, social media, and computer games. Here's how you might reflect such a situation. Pay attention to how the layers of emotions are traversed:

You (Y): "Please put your phone down during dinner."
Miranda (M): [No response. Texts message, concentrating on phone.]
Y: "You are afraid of missing out with your friends online."
M: "Yeah." [Continues to text furiously.]

Y: "You are annoyed that I am asking you to stop."

M: "Yeah. I want to be left alone. You are always telling me what to do."

Y: "You feel disrespected and not listened to. You feel connected to your friends."

M: "Yeah."

Y: "You don't feel loved."

M: "Yeah."

The first layer was not anger or frustration; it was fear. The next layer got you to annoyance and frustrated; then you moved to disrespect and not listened to. Finally, you made the jump to the base layer, feeling unloved. All of this took less than thirty seconds.

Apathy and sullenness are common behaviors. I suspect that children become apathetic and sullen when they do not feel safe. The more you try to push for a connection with the apathetic child, the thicker the wall becomes. Try this approach as an alternative:

You (Y): "What's going on?"

Chris (C): "Nothing. Everything is fine."

Y: "You are angry."

C: [Silence.]

Y: "You are angry and frustrated with school."

C: [Silence.]

Y: "No one likes you, especially your teachers."

C: "Yeah."

Y: "You feel abandoned because no one cares for you."

C: "Yeah."

You may not get a response from a sullen, angry, alienated child. Here's how you know that you are getting through: the child does not leave you. As long as the child is staying close to you and is not trying to "escape," you have his attention. Be patient, affect label no more than thirty seconds, and then drop it. You've done well. The child intuitively knows that you are trying to listen. He craves connection and is afraid of rejection, criticism, or abandonment. Your steadfast focus on him will satisfy his needs.

One of the more aggravating moments in life is when a child attacks back, saying something like "I hate you." This usually follows you saying no to the child. Here's how you might try affect labeling:

Thomas (T) [whining]: "I want FaceTime on my iPad."

You (Y): "No. You can't."

T: "I hate you."

Y: "You are angry and frustrated. You are sad."

T: "I never get to have any fun."

Y: "You feel left out and alone."

T: "Pleeeeeease let me have FaceTime."

Y: "You don't feel like you are being listened to."

T: "Yeah. You never listen to me."

Y: "You never feel listened to."

T [sharply nodding]: "Yeah!"

You may have an urge to fix things. This urge arises from your own anxiety around being unloved, unworthy, being judged, and rejected. If you are not aware of your anxiety, you will unconsciously try to "solve" the other's problem to make you feel better. When you succumb to this urge, you engage in emotional invalidation, which is the opposite of affect labeling. I talk more about emotional invalidation further into this chapter. For now, resist your urge to fix things. Focus on listening to and responding to your child's emotional experience.

Emotional Resistance

Another common behavior is resistance to a check-in. You have asked your child whether she has brushed her teeth, cleaned her room, or done her homework. Her response is a grunt, and you become very frustrated. Here's another way to do it using affect labeling:

> **You (Y):** "Have you brushed your teeth?"
> **Marian (M):** "Ugh."
> **Y:** "You are frustrated and feel disrespected."
> **M:** "Ugh."
> **Y:** "You feel controlled without any freedom."
> **M:** "Yep."
> **Y:** "You don't feel like you are being listened to. You feel like no one cares how you feel."
> **M:** "Yeah."

At some point, your child will push back against your affect labeling. This is normal. You are acting differently, which is scary. Your child will be suspicious and fearful of being manipulated. More deeply, your child will feel vulnerable and unsafe as you peel back his or her emotional experience. This is how you deal with it:

> **You (Y):** "You are frustrated."
> **Rick (R):** "Stop doing that stuff to me. You are doing it again!"
> **Y:** "You don't feel listened to."
> **R:** "I told you to stop it! I hate that!"
> **Y:** "You are angry and annoyed."
> **R:** "Yeah. I want you to leave me alone."
> **Y:** "You feel disrespected and want to be left alone."
> **R:** "Yeah."

You don't need to stay with the emotional reflection for very long. If you keep getting pushback, you might be trying too hard. Give it a rest for a day or so. Next time you affect label, make it a one-line throwaway, spoken casually and conversationally. If you are subtle enough, your child will not pick up on it.

You may also want to teach your child what you are doing and why. As children learn how to affect label others, they build their own emotional intelligence and empathic listening, which leads to higher emotional granularity. You can practice and role-play with each other as a way of feeling safer and more connected.

As a means of developing your confidence, write out a typical challenging conversation with your child just like the scenarios before. In the "You" column, write out the emotions he or she experienced as if you were affect labeling your child. Write out his probable responses and continue until you get to the bottom of his emotional experience. This mental rehearsal will make the live-fire exercise more likely to succeed on your first attempt.

A Word on Children with Special Needs

Affect labeling generally works well with special needs kids. Here's a story a colleague, Larry Bridgesmith, sent me about his grandson, who has Asperger's, after Larry attended my workshop:

> [He] immediately flew into a rage last week because his sister appeared to "get credit" for a comment the two of them made at the same time. [My wife] Linda had listened closely to my description of your teaching, and she said to our grandson, "You feel you haven't been listened to." He immediately affirmed her statement, and then she said, "That makes you feel bad." Within ten seconds, the micro-intervention you taught us restored calm and reduced a normally escalating set of circumstances into a calm that might otherwise have taken hours to achieve.

Every child is different and faces his or her unique challenge. Don't hesitate to try affect labeling and be sensitive to the child's reaction.

The Dangers of Emotional Invalidation

Emotional invalidation is the opposite of affect labeling. Instead of acknowledging a child's emotions without criticism or judgment, an adult invalidates and ridicules. Sadly, emotional invalidation is pervasive in our society and culture. The damage it causes is deadly and insidious. In its extreme, it creates violent and dangerous situations.

Emotional invalidation is one of the most lethal forms of childhood emotional abuse. It kills confidence, creativity, and individuality. It shuts down the thinking part of your child's brain, thus inhibiting reasoning, problem-solving, rationality, and nonimpulsive decision-making. Here is a typical example:

> **Father (F):** "How was school today?"
> **Eric (E):** "It sucked. Billy beat me up."
> F: "It couldn't have been that bad."
> E: "All the kids made fun of me."
> F: "I guess you will just have to deal with it."
> E: [Starts to cry a little.]
> F: "Don't be a girl. Stop crying and buck up. Life is tough, and you have to be tougher."

This innocuous-appearing conversation was emotionally brutalizing the boy. Think about some of the lessons he has just learned:

- I can't be honest with Dad because he puts me down.
- Dad doesn't love me.

- My feelings don't matter.
- I hurt, and no one is around to comfort me.
- I am a bad person.
- I will just have to depend on myself and be a rock.
- If life is tough, I will be tougher and meaner than anyone else.
- The world is a bad place to live, and there is no room for softness or love.

How is this boy going to be when he tries his first romantic relationship in ten years? If he has been fed a steady dose of emotional invalidation, we can be assured that he will be emotionally unavailable. He will be lucky to be in a relationship that might work. The seeds of emotional disaster are planted at a very young age, and sadly this is the case especially for men.

We regularly invalidate children's emotions because we ourselves were, and are, often invalidated, so it has become habitual. Some people justify emotional invalidation as teaching life's lessons early or toughening up kids for reality. Don't be fooled. Those are rationalizations and excuses by people who have been deeply wounded by emotional invalidation themselves. There are plenty of positive, powerful ways to raise strong, resilient children. Beating them up emotionally is not one of them.

Emotional invalidation occurs whenever:

- We are told we shouldn't feel the way we feel.
- We are dictated not to feel the way we feel.
- We are told we are too sensitive, too "dramatic," or "high maintenance."
- We are ignored.
- We are judged.
- We are led to believe there is something wrong with us for feeling how we feel.

Here are some example statements of emotional invalidation. Do any of them sound familiar? How many times have you had someone emotionally invalidate you? How many times have you invalidated the emotions of your partner, your children, or yourself?

Get over it.
Grow up.
Don't cry.
Don't be sad.
Stop whining.
Deal with it.
Don't be so dramatic.
Stop being so emotional. Stop feeling sorry for yourself.
You are so stupid.
I'm so stupid.

Each person's feelings are real. Rejecting, invalidating, or minimizing a person's feelings is rejecting that person's reality. What's worse, the evidence shows that childhood emotional abuse, even as "benign" as emotional invalidation, is just as damaging as physical abuse or sexual abuse. Emotional invalidation is a social epidemic that spans generations, and the cost of this epidemic has only recently begun to be understood.

The ACE Study, the Adverse Childhood Experiences Study, is the first large-scale study of a human population looking at the effect of childhood abuse on adult disease and mortality. The ACE Study is based at Kaiser Permanente's San Diego Health Appraisal Center, where more than forty-five thousand adults undergo medical examinations each year.

The ACE Study researchers capitalized on this enormous wealth of data by mailing out questionnaires to the members who had completed the examination process. The form included questions about childhood abuse and household dysfunction. An ACE was any one instance of abuse, which included emotional invalidation and benign emotional neglect as well as physical and sexual abuse, alcoholism, addiction, and incarcerated parents. The researchers compared the medical health information for each of the respondents and compared the information concerning childhood abuse and exposure to family dysfunction. The results were sobering.

The first finding was that 11 percent of the respondents reported psychological abuse, 11 percent reported physical abuse, and 22 percent reported sexual abuse as children. More than 50 percent of the respondents reported at least one ACE. Slightly more than 25 percent of the respondents reported two to four ACEs.

ACEs were very strong predictors of adult health risks and disease and were implicated in the ten leading causes of death in the United States. The researchers discovered a strong relationship between ACEs and heart disease, cancer, chronic bronchitis or emphysema, hepatitis or jaundice, skeletal fractures, and poor self-rated health.

The links between ACEs and physical disease centered on behaviors such as smoking, alcohol or drug abuse, overeating, or sexual behaviors that are adopted to cope with the stress of emotional abuse, domestic violence, or other forms of family and household dysfunction. If a person experienced four or more ACEs, he or she was many times more likely to smoke, be addicted, suffer from depression, suffer from other mental illness, have problems holding a job, and be homeless.[9]

The key takeaway is that most childhood abuse is primarily emotional in nature. We think of sexual or physical abuse as being horrible and don't always consider that subtle emotional abuse is traumatizing too. Merely living with an alcoholic is sufficiently abusive to create an ACE. Emotionally unavailable or inconsistent parenting creates an ACE. Emotional invalidation creates an ACE. The list goes on, and high levels of exposure to ACEs produced anxiety, anger, and depression in children. Oftentimes, ACEs occur in perfectly respectable homes. They are just as likely to occur in upper socioeconomic families as in poverty-stricken families.

For the next forty-eight hours, pay attention to emotional invalidation. Where is it occurring? Who is invalidating whom? Did you catch yourself invalidating someone? Did someone invalidate you? As you pay attention, you will witness how pervasive this is. Because it seems "normal," no one challenges it. Emotional invalidation is not a cause célèbre like removing landmines or ending polio. It just is. And it is time to stop it.

You have the tools for stopping this everyday cruelty and abuse. Affect labeling is the antidote. Like any antidote, it is up to you to use it. I am hopeful you and millions like you will do just that. Our children and families will be so much healthier and happier.

Chapter Summary

In this chapter, we applied basic affect labeling to a number of common and aggravating behaviors with young children. Here are the takeaways:

- Affect labeling children is usually quick.
- The difference between affect labeling and other responses is that you are focusing on your child's emotional experience until he or she calms down.
- You must be patient and nonjudgmental.
- Emotions come in layers; you work through the layers as they present themselves.
- Empathic listening is the ability to read the emotional data field of another, interpret the data, and respond with appropriate affect labeling.

- Feeling unloved is at the bottom of most escalated behavior.
- Emotional invalidation is the norm. It is toxic and abusive to everyone, especially to children.
- The ACE Study demonstrates the long-term devastation of emotional abuse. Even the most benign abuse is dangerous. The antidote is awareness and affect labeling.

3

After Restoring the Calm, Then What?

My ten-year-old granddaughter was going through some anger outbursts that left her mother and I crazed. She would get angry and shut down no matter what we said or asked her to do, down to brushing her teeth. For over a year there were a lot of tears and yelling that never accomplished anything but much frustration for all of us. Just trying to get this child dressed would turn into a horrible three-hour screaming match.

After being introduced to Doug's work, we thought, what the heck, let's give this a try. Anything had to be better than feeling like we lived in a war zone. Although very apprehensive about something that just seemed to be a new way to talk to a child, my daughter and I read over the new language and began. I must say, from the moment we said the first thing to my granddaughter on that very night, everything changed. When she got angry over having to go to bed, our response was "You seem angry. Can you tell us why you're angry?" And, poof, what was in the past the start of her screaming, "Just leave me alone," turned into her whole story about why she hated the feel of her sheets and could not sleep. Something so easy to remedy, and we did that night. Who knew that a ten-year-old could be that sensitive?

The next day again trying to get her dressed for school, she shut down and started to cry. Her mom said, "You seem sad. Why are you crying?" And out it came: all of this stuff about how her clothes made her skin hurt. The pain that she was in just wearing socks and shoes. We found out by simply listening to her emotions that for years she had been suffering from a condition called hypersensitivity. We would have had no idea what something as simple as wearing tight socks truly felt like to her. Being parents, we had assumed it had to do with her not wanting to go to school. Or maybe she did not get along with the kids at school.

The biggest aha moment after starting the de-escalating protocol was realizing that every time we would fight with her it was about us. The "I" feel, "I" need, not what she was really feeling. Now we live in a home where when someone gets upset, it's up, out, and done. We communicate freely and have now taught my granddaughter the same skills, and they work so well we know it will change her future in communicating in any situation.

—**Devra Jacobs**

The Range of Problem-Solving Possibilities

Obviously, calming someone down does not mean the problem is solved. However, you cannot begin to have a conversation about problem-solving with someone who is upset and highly emotional. Emotions arise to make us pay attention to our environment. The more emotional our experience, the less we can think clearly, resist impulses, and engage in constructive problem-solving. Only after calm is restored can we begin to address the issue with the rational part of the brain.

There is a broad range of problem-solving processes, from least coercive to most coercive. Most people resort to coercive decision-making as their default. Usually, coercion is the first conflict resolution process experienced as a child, and children learn quickly that the person who has the most power wins. Coercion may be effective in the short term. However, it always carries costs, many of them hidden.

If you can solve problems without coercion, the solutions usually stick. Knowing how to solve problems quickly and efficiently without coercion is the trick. In this chapter, we look at three problem-solving skills that are generally more effective than coercion:[10]

1. Reflective Listening
2. Results-Based Coaching
3. Accountable Agreements

Reflective Listening

There are four levels of reflective listing:

1. Simple Reflecting or Mirroring
2. Paraphrasing
3. Reflecting Core Messaging
4. Affect Labeling

Each level of listening is powerful when used appropriately. The problem is that most people tend to use reflection or mirroring and paraphrasing in de-escalation situations, and that just does not work. However, mirroring and paraphrasing are critical when both people need to be clear about what information or request is being exchanged.

Simple Reflecting or Mirroring

This is the most basic acknowledgement of what a person has just said. It is restating the words the speaker said without adding anything additional. At this level of listening, we are focusing on the words, not on the emotions. Sometimes, through use of a subtle change in words, a simple reflection can accomplish a shift in emphasis.

Speaker: "She is driving me crazy, trying to get me to quit."
You: "She is driving you crazy, trying to get you to quit."
Speaker: "I don't have anything to say."
You: "You don't have anything to say."

There are other times when mirroring is critical. For example, I am an instrument-rated pilot. If I file an instrument flight plan to fly from Los Angeles to San Francisco, I must receive an oral clearance from an air traffic controller before I taxi to the runway. The air traffic controller will read the clearance to me, which I must copy down and then read back verbatim to the controller. If I get it wrong, the controller will correct me until I get it right. If I get it right the first time, the controller will say, "Read back correct." We both then know what I am expected to do when airborne. Obviously, this clarity prevents pieces of aluminum moving along in excess of two hundred miles an hour from colliding with each other in the sky.

You will find read-backs and mirroring effective in ordinary life, especially when making agreements and setting expectations. People will find it a little bizarre when you "read back" what has been agreed to. However, you would be amazed at how many conflicts you can avoid by spending a couple of extra seconds getting clarity at the outset.

Do not use simple reflection or mirroring to de-escalate strong emotions. Most people have unconsciously learned some sort of reflective listening, involving words as a means of calming people down. We know from experience, however, that when we are mirroring people who are upset, they tend to become angrier.

Paraphrasing

With this type of reflection, you reflect back what the person said as a paraphrase.

> **Speaker**: "She is driving me crazy, trying to get me to quit."
> **You**: "Her methods are really bothering you."
> **Speaker**: "I don't have anything to say."
> **You**: "You're not feeling talkative today."

Paraphrasing is a good way to show that you understood the meaning of what was communicated without mimicking back what was said. Like mirroring, paraphrasing is not an effective tool for de-escalating strong emotions. It is, however, very useful in communicating that you understand the meaning of the words.

Reflecting the Core Message

With this reflection, you are going beyond the spoken words to get to the deeper message the speaker is trying to convey. Oftentimes, people ramble on and on, not sure what they are trying to say. They simply talk out loud, flitting from idea to idea as each appears in the consciousness. If you try to mirror or paraphrase this conversation, you must have a phenomenal memory to be successful. Thus, you could use the skill of core messaging to go right to the heart of what the speaker has been trying to say for the last half hour.

Reflecting the core message helps the speaker gain clarity and provides a deep emotional satisfaction at having been heard. Core messaging is taken up in more detail in chapter 5.

Speaker: "It would stink to have to lose my house, but no way do I want to have to pay for it while she's living in it with her boyfriend."
You: "The injustice you are experiencing is painful."
Speaker: "It would be so hard to settle with all of my debt hanging over me."
You: "You wonder how you are going to get through all of this."

Affect Labeling

This is the deepest level of reflection, and was introduced in chapters 1 and 2.

Speaker: "It would stink to have to lose my house, but no way do I want to have to pay for it while she's living in it with her boyfriend."
You: "You are angry, frustrated, and sad. You feel betrayed and disrespected. You feel grief and abandonment."
Speaker: "It would be so hard to settle with all of my debt hanging over me."
You: "You are anxious and fearful. You are confused and uncertain. You feel alone and unsupported. You feel abandoned."

Affect labeling is the go-to form of reflective listing when you have to calm an angry person down. No other form of listening will be as effective as affect labeling.

Results-Based Coaching

Results-based coaching is a skill used to help other people solve problems. In this situation, your need to be heard is low, and the other person's need to be heard is high. Your job is to help the other person solve a problem without giving any advice. There are three steps to the skill:

1. Define the problem and understand the goals.
2. Explore the possibilities.
3. Agree on an action plan.

In step one, you are listening to your friend or child. If the speaker is upset or angry, you affect label until you calm him or her down. Then, you paraphrase what you understand to be the problem and the goals. The formula is: *So, your problem is* _____, *and your goal is*_____.

The secret is to keep your paraphrase as succinct as possible. This is a form of core messaging that allows the speaker to reflect on what is said. Sometimes the speaker will agree with your paraphrase, sometimes not. Either way, the purpose here is to gain clarity over the speaker's problem and goals. Step one might look like this between you and a friend:

Friend (F): "I have a real problem. Do you have a few minutes to help me?"
You (Y): "Sure."
F: "I have a home in St. Louis. I was renting it out to make some income when my son came to me and asked if he could manage the house for me. Since I live so far away, I thought that might be a good idea, and I could pay him a little bit to take care of everything. Once I gave him permission, he started taking all of the rent from the tenants and isn't giving me any of the money. He is saying that he needs the money to live off of and that I do not need it. I am pretty upset about this because I think I am being disrespected and abused, and I cannot quite decide what to do."

Y: "You're feeling disrespected and betrayed by your son, whom you trusted to take care of the house you own in St. Louis. Your problem is that your son is not paying you any of the rent, and your goal is to figure out a way to get rid of this problem so that it is no longer upsetting you."

F: "Yeah."

In this first step, you listen and affect label until you understand the problem and the goal. Once you have it, you reflect it back. You are not giving any advice, offering any solutions, or trying to fix things. Sometimes, when friends tell us about problems, we feel their anxiety. To soothe ourselves, we jump right into advice-giving and fixing without doing enough listening. Usually, the results are not so great. Either your advice is rejected, or, if followed and it does not work, you are blamed for the outcome.

Step two requires you to ask two simple questions:

What have you tried so far?

What else could you try that you haven't?

Just like in step one, you may not offer any advice or try to fix anything. Your job is to be a sounding board, reflecting back what you have heard. Here's what it looks like:

You (Y): "What have you tried so far?"

Friend (F): "I've asked him to give me the rent money, and he just laughed at me. Haven't done anything else."

Y: "You've asked him for the rent money, and he refused you disrespectfully."

F: "Yeah. He pissed me off. My own son!"

Y: "You were pissed off and saddened that your son betrayed you."

F: "Yeah."

Y: "What else could you try that you haven't?"

F: "I could try asking one of my brothers, who lives in St. Louis, to talk to him."

Y: "Good. What else could you try that you haven't?"

F: "I could talk to the tenants and tell them my son is no longer working for me."

Y: "Good. What else could you try that you haven't?"

F: "I could sell the house."

Y: "So, you could have one of your brothers talk some sense into your son. You could tell the tenants to deal directly with you. And you could sell the house. Anything else you can think of?"

F: "No, not really."

It seems so simple: just ask questions and reflect back the answers and emotions. Actually, if you keep your ego out of the conversation, it is simple. The hardest part of problem-solving is keeping you out of it. We are so used to giving unsolicited advice and jumping in to fix things that sitting back and guiding a friend through a simple problem-solving process seems absurd. However, the problem is not yours, and it is not yours to solve or fix. You provide your highest service to your friend when you act as a guide instead of a know-it-all, bossy advice columnist.

Step three is to agree on an action plan. Again, your only job is to ask a question: of the ideas you have come up with, which one seems to be the best?

Your friend will think it over and weigh the options. Usually, one idea will resonate. Let's say that your friend decides that she would be best off selling the house. Now your job is to help her craft a time and action plan that is specific on details. Again, your modus operandi is to question, not to give unsolicited advice. You might start with, "Okay, so your best choice is to sell the house. What are the things you will need to do to sell the house?" This leads into a brainstorming session about finding a real estate agent, getting a listing agreement, notifying the tenants and your son, and so forth. You might even want to write all of this down in the form of an agreement your friend is making with herself.

Once you've listed out the details, your last job is to set a time and place to check back in to see how things are going. By creating an obligation to check in, you are creating a moral imperative for your friend to perform. Procrastination is easy when it comes to hard decisions. By gently, but firmly, holding your friend accountable with a progress meeting, you help her overcome the inertia of the status quo.

If you have gone through steps one and two and your speaker cannot come up with options, you may ask the following question: would you be willing to listen to my advice on this matter?

Observe that you are asking permission to give advice. This is different than how most people give advice. Very few people ask permission; they assume that because they have borne the brunt of the friend's problem, they are entitled to give advice. Not true. You may not assume that a friend talking about a problem is interested in your opinion. Ask for and receive explicit permission. Then, and only then, may you offer up your opinion on what should be done.

The focus of result-based coaching, just like reflective listening and affect labeling, is on the speaker, not on you. The moment an "I" is injected into the process, the likelihood of a good solution for the speaker drops dramatically.

Creating Accountable Agreements

Consider this common situation at home:

You (Y): "Clean up your room."
Your Thirteen-Year-Old (13): "Okay."

Hours go by, and the room still looks like a hand grenade exploded in it. You become frustrated and start yelling at your thirteen-year-old for obedience. Your kid sulks and becomes even more stubborn. What to do?

As crazy as it sounds, the real problem is with you. By failing to reach an accountable agreement with your teenager, you set yourself up for frustration and failure. It's not always good enough to believe that another person knows what your expectations are. Common sense tells us that other people cannot read our minds. Yet we persist in expecting people to understand exactly what we want and how we want things done without asking or seeking clarity.

The solution is to recognize when an accountable agreement is necessary. Making an accountable agreement does not have to be a drawn-out affair. You will find that taking an extra minute to make an agreement will save you hours of grief. As the man said, "Pay me now or pay me later."

An accountable agreement has the following elements:

- The people making the agreement are identified.
- The agreement is specific as to what is to be done and to what standard.
- The agreement is specific as to how performance is to be done.
- The agreement is specific as to when performance is to be accomplished.
- The agreement specifies what happens if there is a failure to perform.

You can make agreements with three-year-olds that work if you make sure that all of these elements are present. Here is how an agreement conversation might go with the thirteen-year-old:

Y: "I need you to clean your room. Let's talk about an agreement."

13: "Okay."

Y: "By a clean room, I mean that your clothes are either put in the hamper for washing or put away in your closet. Hanging clothes should be hung on hangers, and folded clothes should be folded neatly and put in your dresser. Can you repeat back what I just said?"

13: "Yeah. Put the dirty clothes in the hamper, fold and put away my folding clothes in my dresser, and make sure my hanging clothes are hung neatly in the closet."

Y: "Yes. In addition, a clean room means that garbage is put in the wastebasket and removed from the room. Dishes and glasses are returned to the kitchen and are cleaned. Games and toys are put away neatly. And your bed is made. Could you repeat that for me?"

13: "You want me to move all the garbage out of the room and take the dirty dishes and glasses to the kitchen and wash them. You want me to put all of my games and toys away and make the bed."

Y: "Yes. Is there anything about what I have asked for that is unreasonable to you?"

13: "No."

Y: "Let us talk about when this might all happen. What would be a reasonable time to get your room clean?"

13: "I could probably do it in the next couple of hours. I have a movie I am watching and can do it after it is over with."

Y: "So, it is one o'clock now. Could you have your room cleaned by four o'clock this afternoon?"

13: "Sure."

Y: "Okay. What might be some of the things that will get in the way of you getting your room cleaned by four o'clock?"

13: "Well, I might forget."

Y: "What can you do to remind yourself to clean your room after you are done watching your movie?"

13: "I can write a big note to myself."

Y: "Okay. What other things might get in the way of cleaning your room by four o'clock?"

13: "I could get distracted."

Y: "That is kind of like forgetting. What could you do to keep you from getting distracted from cleaning a room by four o'clock this afternoon?"

13: "I will not get distracted. I'll do it. I promise."

Y: "One more thing. What should we do if your room is not clean by four o'clock? How would you like me to handle the situation with you?"

13: "Uh, I don't know? I guess you could remind me."

Y: "Tell you what. If I have to remind you to clean your room at four o'clock, you agree that you will do the dishes tonight after dinner."

13: "Yeah, that seems fair."

Y: "Okay. We have agreed that you will clean your room by four o'clock this afternoon after you have watched a movie. We also agreed that a clean room means that your clothes are hung and folded, dirty clothes are put in the hamper, garbage is tossed in the wastebasket and the wastebasket emptied, dirty dishes and glasses are returned to the kitchen and washed, games and toys are put away, and your bed is made. Repeat back for me what we have agreed to just so we both are clear."

13: "I agree that I am gonna clean the room by four o'clock after my movie. I am going to fold and hang my clothes, put my dirty clothes in the hamper, put all the garbage in a wastebasket and empty it, bring the dirty dishes and glasses to the kitchen and wash them, put away my games and toys, and make the bed."

Y: "And if you do not complete cleaning your room by four
o'clock, you agree to do the dishes tonight."

13: "Yeah. If I do not get the room cleaned by four o'clock, I will
have to do dishes tonight as well."

Y: "Great. Thanks a lot."

You might be thinking to yourself, "I do not have time for this. This
is a big pain." Actually, if you get into the habit of making accountable
agreements with those around you for what you want done, you will
find less conflict, less drama, and more happiness all around. A small
investment up front will pay off big dividends later on.

This entire conversation might take three or four minutes.
Despite being short and sweet, a lot went on it. Let's look at it closely.

You open the conversation with a request. When you give
choices to people, especially children, you respect their autonomy.
Once they feel like they have a choice, people are far less likely to
resist, be passive aggressive, or become stubborn.

Once you secure an agreement to have the conversation, you
state your clear expectations about what a clean room means to you.
This requires you to be clear in your mind about what you want. You
might be surprised how often you lack clarity about what you want
and expect other people to figure it out anyway.

You confirm understanding by asking for a mirroring reflection:
"Repeat back what I just asked for." This seems trivial and boring. "Of
course he heard me say the words. What is he, deaf or something?"
you might be thinking. Just because you spoke words does not mean
that another person understood them the way you intended. Using
mirroring and paraphrasing accomplishes two important goals.
First, when the other person successfully repeats back your expectations, you both know that you have clarity. Second, when the other
person repeats back your expectations, she is anchoring the expectation inside herself. This makes accountability more likely.

If the other person can't repeat back your expectation, you have to do it again. Here's what it looks like:

Y: "By a clean room, I mean that your clothes are either put in the hamper for washing or put away in your closet. Hanging clothes should be hung on hangers and folded clothes should be folded neatly and put in your dresser. Can you repeat back what I just said?"

13: "Uh. I forgot."

Y: "By a clean room, I mean that your clothes are either put in the hamper for washing or put away in your closet. Hanging clothes should be hung on hangers and folded clothes should be folded neatly and put in your dresser. Try repeating it back again."

13: "Uh, you want me to get rid of the clothes on the floor."

Y: "You said, 'Get rid of the clothes on the floor.' By a clean room, I mean that your clothes are either put in the hamper for washing or put away in your closet. Hanging clothes should be hung on hangers and folded clothes should be folded neatly and put in your dresser. Try again."

13: "Yeah. You want me to put the dirty clothes in the hamper, fold and put away my folding clothes in my dresser, and make sure my hanging clothes are hung neatly in the closet."

Y: "Yes."

You might have to repeat this process several times with the other person. Do not become frustrated. Do not tell the other person to listen carefully. Do not tell the person he or she is dumb and stupid. Many people, and especially children and teens, have a limited working memory capacity. Their brains fill up with just a thimbleful of information. Once their working memory is at capacity, they physically cannot remember or recall anything further.

By requiring mirroring and paraphrasing, you are helping the other person stretch working memory capacity. You are helping them grow their brain power. This is not so trivial a matter after all! It does require patience on your part. It requires you to be self-aware enough to squash your own frustration and be patient.

Once you have reached an understanding of what is to be done and how it is to be accomplished, you want to agree on a time for completion. Again, ask what is reasonable to the other person. If he proposes something that is not reasonable to you, find out what underlies the proposal. It might go like this:

Y: "Let us talk about when this might all happen. What would be a reasonable time to get your room clean?"
13: "I could probably do it Wednesday afternoon."
Y: "Today is Friday. Why do you think you will need five days to clean your room?"

You might be surprised at the reasonableness of the answer, even if you don't like it:

Y: "Let us talk about when this might all happen. What would be a reasonable time to get your room clean?"
13: "I could probably do it before I go to bed tonight."
Y: "It's 3:00 PM. Why do you think you will need seven hours to clean your room?"
13: "Mom, I have a term paper I'm finishing and need to get to the library. I won't be back until just before dinner. I can clean my room after dinner and after I complete the paper."

If the reason seems like a dodge to get out of the agreement, make your request accompanied by "Is this reasonable?"

Y: "Let us talk about when this might all happen. What would be a reasonable time to get your room clean?"

13: "I could probably do it before I go to bed tonight."

Y: "It's 3:00 PM. Why do you think you will need seven hours to clean your room?"

13: "Um. I just have a lot of other stuff to do."

Y: "I'd like you to have your room cleaned by four o'clock this afternoon. Is that reasonable?"

By asking if your request is reasonable, you are giving the other person a chance to challenge your request as unreasonable. The good thing about this is that it puts the persuasive burden on the other person to explain why you are being unreasonable. The conversation is now a short negotiation over time of performance. Eventually, you will reach agreement.

The next step is one that most everyone misses. Simply ask what might get in the way of performing the agreement on time. It's amazing how powerful this question can be:

Y: "Okay. What might be some of the things that will get in the way of you getting your room cleaned by four o'clock?"

By having a conversation about the possible barriers to completing the agreement, you are problem-solving before the problem arises. When the other person can identify potential obstacles to keeping the agreement, you both can develop strategies beforehand. If you include this in every agreement conversation, the likelihood of promises being kept skyrockets.

Even with potential problems identified, there is always the possibility that the other person will not do what he or she says. A solid agreement conversation will always include a question: "What if you don't perform?" There are consequences to not keeping promises.

Sometimes, the consequences are light; sometimes, they are heavy. If you talk about consequences beforehand, you are likely to see better performance and less resistance to the consequences if they become necessary.

End the agreement conversation with a full-mirrored reflection of the specifics. Keep at it until the other person has mirrored successfully the entire agreement. If it's complicated enough, write out the essential terms of the agreement on a piece of paper and date it. You don't have to sign it as long as you both agree that the agreement in writing is accurate. You are not writing up a complex agreement, so formalities are not necessary. This is a social contract, not a legal contract.

Why go to all this trouble? Why not just yell at your kid to clean the room?

When making agreements with children, you are teaching them how to be responsible. You are teaching them how to seek clarity and how to do what they say they are going to do. In other words, you are teaching them integrity. Every time a child performs an agreement as agreed, the child has learned another lesson about trust, responsibility, and being accountable. Repeated many times over many years, that moral code will be embedded into a young adult. What more could we ask for? It is your job to make this happen.

You are also teaching children how to obtain agreements from others. They will learn from you how to be clear about expectations, how to agree on performance, and how to plan for failure. You are teaching leadership and management skills that will be valuable in the child's adult working life.

There is a funny thing about simple, express agreements. People tend to want to be accountable because they want their self-image and their behaviors to be consistent. If a child sees herself as a person to be liked, she will want to make sure that her actions are consistent with her promises. Accountable agreements have a moral force that is quite powerful. If you can find the discipline within yourself to use this accountable agreement process whenever you want something done by somebody else, you will find that people around you will do what they say more often than not. That is a happy thing.

As an exercise, write out an agreement you would like to have with your child, teenager, or partner. Keep it simple but be very specific. Then, using the format of the scenarios we just discussed, write out how the conversation might go.

Chapter Summary

In this chapter, we have learned some simple problem-solving skills to use after you have calmed an angry, upset, or emotional person. Of course, you can use these skills when de-escalation is not needed. The skills are:

- Four types of reflective listening:

  - Mirroring: Repeating back word for word what another says
  - Paraphrasing: Repeating back what another says in your own words
  - Core Messaging: Summarizing what another is trying to say, usually through metaphor
  - Affect Labeling: Stating the emotions of another in simple, direct "You" statements

- Results-Based Coaching
- Accountable Agreements

4

Minimum Coercion, Maximum Listening

It's been almost two years now since I started [with Prison of Peace], and my life has been completely transformed. I have learned about affect labeling and core messaging, which has helped me to search within myself, giving me a deeper understanding of myself and others. These skills allow me to "listen someone into existence." Many inmates don't feel "listened" to. Prison of Peace's skills validate someone's "emotional reality." Prison of Peace's unique technique provides for de-escalation and the creation of safe, healthy options.

Learning this has enabled me to reengage the long-term rational thinking necessary to increase mental emotional well-being. As a result, I have been able to diminish reactivity and impulsiveness, resulting in a significant decrease in anger and frustration, and I can provide this as a service to others.

—**Daniel Henson**, Valley State Prison

If you have teenagers in your life, this chapter shows you various ways of using the tools in the preceding chapters to calm them down and solve problems with a minimum amount of coercion while increasing your capacity to listen and affect label.

As in chapter 2 on young children, even if you are not a parent or don't currently interact with teenagers, this chapter offers important practice, tools, and tips for when you're confronted with an angry or emotionally charged situation or person, whether a teen or not. You will easily find that these scenarios and conversations can be quite familiar in other areas in life, especially when dealing with anyone who is unresponsive and emotionally resistant. I also share some valuable tips on dealing with bullies, which can happen at any time and at any age, and how to cultivate connection and deep listening through peace circles.

De-escalating Unresponsive Teens

As every adult has experienced, the seven-year passage from age thirteen to nineteen is difficult. For teenagers, the transition from childhood to young adulthood may create intense anxiety, frustration, and confusion. The safety, the security, and the certainties of childhood seem to have disappeared. Teens reach puberty at different ages, which can intensify their feeling of isolation and their anxieties. Self-centeredness is normal as teens are consumed with their own issues:

"Am I normal?"
"How do I look?"
"What do people think about me?"

Teens naturally go inward and withdraw from their families. Teens are not open and frank about what they are experiencing for many reasons, including confusion, embarrassment, self-esteem management (an overwhelming need to look confident and competent), fear of rejection, and fear of humiliation. Teens often give up a great deal of themselves in pursuit of the closeness they crave, only to crash against the hard reality that other teens aren't developmentally able to offer them what they need.

The good news is that teen behaviors fall into predictable, repetitive patterns; they are not inventive in how they cope with life. This predictability gives us opportunities to connect and engage in deeper ways, if we are willing to make the effort.

Most teen behaviors are unconscious and automatic. The brain's executive function does not come online until the midtwenties, so we cannot expect deep reflection and self-awareness from teens. That means that we sometimes have to help them out.

The first rule in de-escalating teens is to check your own attitudes and behaviors. The following unconscious parental behaviors invalidate emotions and are abusive. They drive teens away and escalate emotions. Avoid these behaviors:

- Lecturing
- Reprimanding
- Threatening
- Asking inane questions repeatedly ("How was school today?")
- Cross-examining or interrogating
- Displaying anger, frustration, or resentment

Your job is to be emotionally available for your teen when your teen needs you to be that way. The most important part of staying available is your state of mind. Your child senses your emotional availability. Parents who have close relationships with their teens often say that they've made it a practice to drop everything else if their teens signal a desire to talk. This can be difficult if you're also handling a demanding job and other responsibilities, of course. But kids who feel that other things are more important to their parents often look elsewhere when they're emotionally needy.

Teens think that parents either don't care or don't understand. They appear to say, "Go away; I can do it myself," when they really mean, "Stay close behind me most of the time, beside me some of the time, and in front of me only if you see I'm doing something stupid or self-destructive."

Your challenge is to be understanding and caring without being overbearing, overcontrolling, over-needy, overanxious. You have to hold a presence that is strong and stable without being smothering or stifling. It all boils down to emotional validation and giving a teen a sense that she has some autonomy. Generally, the following guidelines will help you navigate explosive emotional terrain with your teen:

- Find a way to open communication without being demanding or obvious, such as:

  - Use texting to grab attention.
  - Stay up late and "bump" into your teen when she's coming home or doing her homework.
  - Don't interrupt when she is engaged with peers.

- As the listener, your needs are unimportant. Park your ego and dependencies at the door.
- If there is silence, start with a tentative affect label: "You seem angry."
- Affect label for no more than ninety seconds.
- If you get pushback, stop. Retry later and be more subtle.
- Ignore the words. Ignore the words. Ignore the words. And focus on the emotion under them.

Once some calm is restored, think about problem-solving at the least intrusive and coercive level. Start with results-based coaching if the problem does not involve you. Start with accountable agreements if the problem does involve you. You may set boundaries, but always give choices and consequences. Respect autonomy as much as possible within those boundaries.

Emotional invalidation is a real challenge because the teen's anxiety is so intense it makes you itchy. All your unconscious brain wants to do is get rid of that anxiety. So you blurt out some emotionally invalidating statement and blow the whole deal. Learn to live with your teen's intense anxiety. Don't try to fix it. Most important, resist soothing yourself at the expense of your teen.

The Sullen, Unengaged Teen

Teenage boys, without wise guidance, can generally have an overly simplistic view of manhood. They come to believe that being a man means being strong, big, and in control. If they don't have emotional granularity, they are incapable of understanding their emotional experience. When they are humiliated by any authority figure such as a parent or teacher, or are rejected by a romantic interest, they feel small, inadequate, and controlled. A common strategy for dealing with the pain of this humiliation is to withdraw inward, tell yourself that no one cares, that you are a rock and an island, and put up a wall between you and any warmth, love, affection, or other beautiful connection from others. It's safer that way. The risk of pain is too great to do otherwise.

Teenagers find it hard to cry and show their feelings, but they do have particular areas of vulnerability. Their frustration may come out by being sullen, rude, and hostile. Many early-to-mid teenagers want to show a tough exterior because they don't know how to handle themselves in public. How do you act "cool" when you're fearful inside and have no clue who or what you are?

Communicating with a sullen and unengaged teenager challenges your listening skills to their limits. On the one hand, you want to reach out. On the other, you are so frustrated and angry at this kid that you can barely keep yourself together. This is where the cardinal rule will save your bacon: ignore the words.

For the ninety seconds you are in de-escalation mode, you have to ignore the words, the looks, the grunts, the sneers, and the utter and complete disrespect you might face. Otherwise, you will be triggered and sucked into the conflict vortex. You can do no good in there.

Here's how one scenario might play out:

Your fourteen-year-old has made an appearance in the kitchen and is ignoring you and everyone else.

You (Y): "You seem angry."
Your Fourteen-Year-Old (14): [Silence, head down, no eye contact.]
Y: "No one is listening to you and you feel disrespected."
14: [Looks up.]
Y: "No one understands you. You are upset and confused because you feel abandoned and lost."
14: "Yeah. How did you know?"
Y: "You're a little curious and you don't trust that anyone cares."
14: "Yep."
Y: "You are feeling unlovable and unworthy. You are feeling that no one really cares about you."
14: "Yeah."

Be silent and see if your teen offers anything up. Just hold safe space without satisfying your need to fill the silence or reduce the anxiety. If nothing further occurs, give a warm, engaging smile and go on about your business.

This exchange might take fifteen to twenty seconds, and that's all that is called for. You have done some powerful work here without having a "conversation" with your teen. First, you have demonstrated your interest in listening to your teen as opposed to having your own needs met. Second, you have been nonjudgmental and noncritical, meeting your teen's need for respect and autonomy. Third, your affect labeling has categorized your teen's experiences for him in a way he could not organize for himself. You expanded his brain power a little. If this is repeated a few times a week, you are likely to see your teen open up a little at a time. When he feels safe, he will engage in conversation and maybe even be ready for some results-based coaching.

Pushback and Resistance

Another response might be pushback to your affect labeling. Depending on your instincts, you may handle this resistance several ways:

Y: "You seem angry."

14: [Silence, head down, no eye contact.]

Y: "No one is listening to you, and you feel disrespected."

14: "Don't do that to me!"

He is not rejecting you; this encounter is not about you. Get over it. This is a young man trying to figure out what he is feeling, wondering why he is so messed up, and experiencing shame because feeling lonely, confused, and inarticulate does not measure up to what he thinks a strong, independent man should be like. Since he lacks any skill at expressing himself, his only avenue to reduce his anxiety and express his frustration is to lash out. This behavioral pattern is common. Many parents listen to the words, are sucked into the conflict, and lose their ability to calm things down. They cannot see the pattern, as obvious as it is, and therefore cannot respond to it nonreactively.

One way to respond to pushback is to persist a little to see what happens:

Y: "You seem angry."
14: [Silence, head down, no eye contact.]
Y: "No one is listening to you, and you feel disrespected."
14: "Don't do that to me!"
Y: "You are confused and frustrated. You don't feel heard or understood."
14: [Silence.]

Silence is always a good response. As long as your teen does not get up and leave, you are making progress. Never, ever give up in the face of silence. You are being tested for your sincerity in trying to reach out. Your teen's brain is unconsciously processing the basic question of whether you are safe or dangerous. Your response to silence is to continue affect labeling a little bit more to see if you can get a head nod, verbal response, and relaxation response. If after one or two more labeling attempts, your teen is still silent, congratulate yourself on establishing a silent connection. Watch out for your anxiety about the silence. If you are not aware of it, your anxiety might cause you to stop affect labeling and say something counterproductive.

Here's another, more difficult, possibility:

Y: "You seem angry."
14: [Silence, head down, no eye contact.]
Y: "No one is listening to you and you feel disrespected."
14: "Don't do that to me!"
Y: "You are confused and frustrated. You don't feel heard or understood."
14: "Would you quit doing that sh*t to me? You aren't my therapist, and I hate this touchy-feely crap you always try on me!"

Seems like you escalated his emotions rather than de-escalating the problem. Maybe. If you made him angrier, calmly back off. There will be plenty of other opportunities. There is no failure here, just a slight shift in tactics. In the face of this anger, you could persist:

Y: "You seem angry."

14: [Silence, head down, no eye contact.]

Y: "No one is listening to you and you feel disrespected."

14: "Don't do that to me!"

Y: "You are confused and frustrated. You don't feel heard or understood."

14: "Would you quit doing that sh*t to me? You aren't my therapist, and I hate this touchy-feely crap you always try on me!"

Y: "You are really angry right now because no one can possibly understand you. You are frustrated by that and feel completely abandoned and alone."

14: [Silence.]

Good job! Silence is golden. You nailed it with that last affect label. Not feeling understood leads to intense loneliness and despair over feeling abandoned. This is a very common experience for modern teens. In fact, it is almost universal.

Suppose your teen goes the other way:

Y: "You seem angry."

14: [Silence, head down, no eye contact.]

Y: "No one is listening to you and you feel disrespected."

14: "Don't do that to me!"

Y: "You are confused and frustrated. You don't feel heard or understood."

14: "Would you quit doing that sh*t to me? You aren't my therapist, and I hate this touchy-feely crap you always try on me!"

Y: "You are really angry right now because no one can possibly understand you. You are frustrated by that and feel completely abandoned and alone."

14: "I hate you. I hate everything about this place!"

Now some real emotions are surfacing. Do you have the courage and love to stand in the middle of this emotional chaos your teen is in and hold a safe space for him? Here's a potential response that I particularly like:

Y: "You seem angry."

14: [Silence, head down, no eye contact.]

Y: "No one is listening to you and you feel disrespected."

14: "Don't do that to me!"

Y: "You are confused and frustrated. You don't feel heard or understood."

14: "Would you quit doing that sh*t to me? You aren't my therapist, and I hate this touchy-feely crap you always try on me!"

Y: "You are really angry right now because no one can possibly understand you. You are frustrated by that and feel completely abandoned and alone."

14: "I hate you. I hate everything about this place!"

Y: "You are really angry and upset. I am going to sit here and hold a safe and loving space for you to be as angry, hateful, and upset as you need to be. Dive into your hatred and make it even stronger and more intense. I will be here for as long as you need to experience all of it."

You are accepting your teen's hatred, which is very real in this moment, and you are not running. You are declaring your intention to hold a safe and loving space. You are doing something surprising and counterintuitive: you are inviting your teen to experience that hatred intensely, even increase it, if that's what he needs to do. You are not frightened, angry, put off, or upset. You are calm and loving. Just sit there for your teen. This is when miracles may occur. Don't be surprised if this happens:

Y: "You seem angry."
14: [Silence, head down, no eye contact.]
Y: "No one is listening to you and you feel disrespected."
14: "Don't do that to me!"
Y: "You are confused and frustrated. You don't feel heard or understood."
14: "Would you quit doing that sh*t to me? You aren't my therapist, and I hate this touchy-feely crap you always try on me!"
Y: "You are really angry right now because no one can possibly understand you. You are frustrated by that and feel completely abandoned and alone."
14: "I hate you. I hate everything about this place!"
Y: "You are really angry and upset. I am going to sit here and hold a safe and loving space for you to be as angry, hateful, and upset as you need to be. Dive into your hatred and make it even stronger and more intense. I will be here for as long as you need to experience all of it."
14: "I hate you. I hate you. I hate Mom. I hate everyone. I hate school."
Y: "You hate everyone and everything." [Pause reflectively.] "Do you hate the dog?"
14: [Laughing.] "No, I don't hate the dog. And I don't hate you or Mom or school or anyone else. Thanks for listening to me."
Y: "You're welcome."

You do break a rule, in a way, by asking a question. However, the question isn't about whether or what emotion is being experienced.

It is a question about a possible object of hatred that you know cannot possibly exist. The humor you inject breaks the spell.

The tactic is to permit and embrace the strong emotions. Tell your teen to experience that emotion deeply. Affect label it a little and take it out to a humorous extreme if the timing seems right.

Instant Gratification

Your sixteen-year-old daughter, Kelsey, is annoyed that she has to drive the beat-up old Chevy to school:

Kelsey (K): "I don't want to be seen in this piece of junk! Have you seen what kinds of cars the other kids drive!?"

Y: "You are annoyed and embarrassed that you have to drive the old Chevy to school."

K: "It is so uncool. I will look like a nerdy jerk."

Y: "You are afraid that other kids will think you are a nerdy jerk, and no one will like you."

K: "Who would like some idiot who drives a car like that?"

Y: "You are anxious that you might be made fun of and humiliated by your friends."

K: "Yeah."

That was a pretty fast de-escalation. Let's help her out with some results-based coaching:

Y: "Want some help figuring out what to do?"

K: "What I really want is a cool-looking new car."

Y: "If you were to have a really cool-looking new car to drive to school, what would be all of the good things that would happen to you?"

K: "Uh, well, I guess people would think that I am really cool."

Y: "And if people thought you were really cool, what would be all of the good things that would happen to you?"

K: "I would be liked and respected. And have a lot of friends. And guys would want to date me."

Y: "Good. If you were liked and respected and attractive to the guys, what good things would happen to you?"

K: "Um, I guess I would feel really good and be happy."

Y: "Now you're talking. Your goal is to feel good and be happy."

K: "Yeah."

The results-based coaching conversation starts differently this time. Kelsey is afraid that she will look nerdy and stupid driving the old beater to school. She takes a position that a cool-looking new car is the solution to her problem. Your job is to find out what her real goals are. Adults and kids alike will state a position, "I want X," without thinking through their real needs. By asking the simple question, "What are all the good things that would happen to you if you had a cool car?" you help Kelsey think about her true needs.

As this conversation unfolds, you keep Kelsey digging until you find her real interest: to be happy, respected, and attractive. At that point, you move into the second step of results-based coaching by asking, "What kinds of positive things are you doing to feel good about yourself and be happy?" After Kelsey answers that question, you ask, "What else could you think of doing that would make you happy and feel good about yourself?" This moves Kelsey into problem-solving mode and then into an action plan. The cool-car thing is long forgotten as Kelsey sees the real problem and the real solutions open to her.

Any time your teen makes a demand ("I want"), you can use this tactic to help her find out what it is that is truly important to her. The total investment of your time will be less than ten minutes in most cases. Repeat this exercise a few times and your teen will quickly figure out how to do it on her own. The whining should simmer down.

Bullying

Teenage bullying isn't always physical. Verbal and emotional bullying can be as traumatic as physical bullying. As a victim of bullying, your teen is unlikely to want to confide in you. Like all victims, he or she will feel humiliated, incompetent, and ashamed. Since the dominant concerns for a teenager are looking competent, being in control, and being liked, the perceived weakness of being a bullied victim is not easily admitted. Like all victims, a bullied teenager needs to be heard at a deep, emotional level. She does not need advice or problem solving.

Let's assume that your teen has been bullied and wants to talk to you about it. She is very upset. Here's one way to listen to her:

Your Teen (T): "There is a girl in my class who is horrible to me. Every day, she is cruel to me. Calling me things like 'stupid', 'ugly', saying, 'You have no friends', 'No one loves you.'"
You (Y): "You are angry and deeply hurt."
T: "Yes. When I told the counselors about the bullying, they told me, 'Get over it. It happens to everyone. Girls are just being girls.'"
Y: "You don't feel safe and feel betrayed by your counselor."
T: "I complained to the principal. He didn't do anything about it."
Y: "You felt ignored and invisible and completely abandoned."
T: "Yeah."
Y: "All of the adults are ignoring you and allowing the girl to keep bullying you."
T: "Yeah."
Y: "This whole thing is really depressing and sad because no one cares for you."
T: "Yeah."
Y: "Anything else?"
T: "I just want it to stop. I am tired of feeing scared all the time."

Y: "You are tired of being scared and just want to be left alone in peace."

T: "Yeah."

If you think she has felt deeply listened to and understood, you could move into results-based coaching and help her work out some new strategies. The one thing you do not do is get angry about her apparent lack of protection from the school authorities. Our instinct is to jump up, call the principal, and raise holy hell. Most of the time, this solves nothing and creates more chaos. A deliberate, empathic approach that helps your daughter solve the problem on her own terms is superior to helicoptering in and saving the day. You might soothe your anxieties, but you will not be helping your daughter cope with the bullies of the world. This will not be the last one she encounters. Your strongest and wisest approach is to make sure she is deeply heard and understood by you. That, by itself, will create a sense of safety that will be empowering.

Listening to a Bully

Bullies are made, not born, and come in all shapes and sizes and genders. They typically:

- Have average or above-average self-esteem
- Find satisfaction from causing harm to others
- Seek attention or acceptance from peers
- Seek to make themselves look tough and in charge
- Have little empathy toward their victims or others
- Seek to dominate other people or situations
- Are described as hot-tempered and impulsive

Bullies are often self-centered in that they are concerned with only their own needs and pleasures. They frequently do not accept responsibility for their behavior or the consequences of their bullying.

Bullying may be common among students who come from abusive homes or where physical punishment is frequently employed. Students frequently model behavior observed within their home environment, including abusive behavior exhibited by parents to each other or toward others. They dominate weaker kids because the act of domination gives them a dopamine rush in their brains. They feel pleasure at being on top and "better" than their victims. Unfortunately, the pleasure wears off quickly, and the bully has to find another victim to get the high again. In a certain way, it's an addiction acquired to cope with the pain of a deeper wound.

Suppose a teen is a bully. An opportunity arises for you to explore bullying behavior with this teen. How would you handle it? Would you try to soothe your own anxiety by blaming and shaming, or would you find out what is going on at a deeper level?

Here is one way you might approach a teen bully:

You (Y): "You were bullying Skyler at school. Tell me what happened."

Marissa (M): "It was nothing. Me and my friends were just having some fun. We didn't mean anything by it."

Y: "You are annoyed at having been caught and are afraid of what might happen."

M: "Not afraid of anything. "

Y: "No one listens to you and you feel like everyone is against you."

M: "Yeah."

Y: "You are angry."

M: "Yeah."

Y: "Bullying Skyler made you feel strong."

M: "I didn't bully her."

Y: "Well, teasing Skyler made you look good in front of your friends."

M: "We were just having fun."

Y: "You enjoyed yourself."

M: "Yeah.

Y: "It made you feel good."

M: "Yeah, it was fun."

Y: "Skyler is not important to you."

M: "She's just a nerdy little freshman who wears weird glasses. No one likes her."

Y: "You felt safe picking on Skyler because you didn't think she would fight back."

M: "No way."

Y: "You like being popular at school."

M: "Yeah."

Y: "You are afraid that if you lose your popularity, no one will want to be with you. You are afraid of feeling abandoned and alone."

M: "Yeah."

This is a tough conversation. Marissa is in general denial, although she offers some justifications to minimize her bullying. She has no interest in personal accountability. As an adult listener, this is maddening, insulting, and frustrating. Her lack of accountability may be interpreted by you as disrespectful and insolent. If you take the bait, your anger and frustration will escalate a bad situation to worse. The best you can expect is to dig into what Marissa might be experiencing emotionally.

As this scenario plays out, you find that Marissa's emotions are all over the place. She is angry, frustrated, annoyed, self-satisfied, afraid, lonely, and happy at her popularity, one after the other. While there is no aha moment, by affect labeling instead of lashing out, you might have helped Marissa develop a bit more emotional granularity. Repeated over time, this type of listening will only have a positive effect.

Just because you are affect labeling to reflect Marissa's emotions does not mean that there are no consequences. What is important is that the consequences be delivered when you are both calm. Consequences delivered in anger will be interpreted as abusive, unfair, and unjustified, and will lose any value as being a part of a teaching moment.

Fostering Peace Circles

What could be done about Marissa's bullying of Skyler? One powerful tool for dealing with a group issue is a process known as a peace circle. Peace circles have been around for as long as humans have sat in a circle and talked. There is something primal about the process that makes it sacred. They are easy to set up and run, if you are willing to be a wise leader. Here's how we teach the process:

The circle is composed of at least five people seated in chairs in a circle. On the floor in the center is some object that can help focus attention. Flowers, candles, a book, or a small statuette are all common centerpieces. You need a talking stick, which can be a feather, a pen, or a small stuffed toy. A circle keeper is designated, who invites people in. Generally, the keeper's job is to ask the guiding questions and keep the ground rules. The ground rules are simple:

- Only the person with the talking piece can speak.
- Before speaking, you must reflect the thoughts and emotions of the previous speaker.
- You may pass and not say anything.
- Limit your thoughts to about ninety seconds.
- Allow the keeper to intervene to keep the flow going smoothly.

The keeper asks three guiding questions, one at a time, allowing everyone in the circle to answer the posed question before moving on. The questions move from the broad to the actionable. For a circle on bullying, the keeper might ask:

1. What is bullying?
2. How does bullying show up at school?
3. What can you do about bullying starting tomorrow?

The person to the keeper's left starts by answering the first question. The person on her left reflects back her thoughts and feelings. If the speaker agrees that the reflection is accurate, the new speaker "earns her turn" to speak. Proceed around the circle. Once everyone has answered the question, the keeper asks the next question, and the process repeats. Repeat again with the third question and the discussion is complete. I like to sit in silence for a minute or two to let the experience settle in before releasing the circle.

To get through to Marissa, I would consider convening a circle of her peers. If I could, I would include Skyler. However, I would only include Skyler with her permission and making sure that she feels absolutely and unconditionally safe.

This simple process is very different from ordinary conversation. A peace circle consists of 98 percent listening and 2 percent talking. It has built-in reflection and affect labeling so every participant experiences being heard deeply. Participation develops discipline and focus. It also fosters empathy and understanding.

If you want to experiment with it, try it at home with your family. Instead of the usual three questions, just ask two questions:

1. What was the best thing that happened to you today?
2. What are you looking forward to tomorrow?

Even three-year-olds can answer these simple questions. Be sure that each speaker is affect labeled and paraphrased. Add a ground rule about mobile devices: they are not allowed in the circle. The whole thing will take fifteen minutes or less and is a great thing to do just before dinner.

Peace circles have universal application in life. Whether prison inmates or business teammates, participating in a circle on a regular basis promotes trust, leadership, understanding, and group cohesion. It is a powerful family tool and is just as powerful in any situation where a group must work together toward a common task or goal.

Chapter Summary

In this chapter, you learned some strategies for listening to teens. The most important points are:

- Ignore the words.
- Listen for and guess at the teen's emotions.
- Be patient.
- Be nonjudgmental.
- Don't soothe yourself at the expense of the teen.
- Listen and affect label bullying.
- Use peace circles to foster understanding and create connections.

5

The Art of Core Messaging

Prison of Peace has had a strange effect on my life as a life-term inmate. Before Prison of Peace, I tended to mind my own business and keep my head down for my own safety. This philosophy kept me safe, but I had very little peace or purpose in my life. Most inmates live this way... just trying to survive. So, I was living in safety, but with a great deal of stress.

Now, there is still a lot of violence that occurs in prison, mostly due to disrespect and miscommunication. This is the exact area I learned to reflect and listen to. Prison of Peace taught me to go behind the words and masks. I am learning to see the real issues and conflicts, and I am given a chance to prevent violence by practicing the mediation skills given to me.

Furthermore, I have tried to find ways to give back to society and make amends with respect to my victims. There is no better way that I can think of to do this than to prevent victims from being created through violence. I truly feel I am preventing conflicts and violence. This has created the sense of purpose I was lacking before. Hopefully, society will be better off because I taught another inmate to make a choice for peace rather than violence.

—**Joseph Harmon**, Valley State Prison

This chapter teaches you how to apply your new skills and knowledge with upset or angry friends. All of us have been with friends who have problems. They turn to us for support and advice, and as caring friends, we listen. Sometimes, they talk on and on, looping around, zigzagging here and there so that following their train of thought is difficult. As much as we care, our foot is tapping. We start to think, "Will he ever get to the point?" When you want to de-escalate a friend, or anyone in this condition, you will find core messaging coupled with affect labeling to be effective at getting to the gist of the issue.

How to Core Message Effectively

Core messaging is the third level of reflective listening. Unlike mirroring (level 1) and paraphrasing (level 2), when you core message, you are not listening to the words being spoken. Instead, you are listening for the deeper meaning the speaker is trying to convey.

Upset people often cannot formulate for themselves what they are meaning to say. They ramble on and on, not even knowing that they are in stream-of-consciousness mode. This is called associative processing, and it occurs when one idea triggers another idea, which triggers something completely different, which diverges onto another thought, and so forth. Essentially, the autonomous part of the speaker's decision-making system is spewing forth whatever comes to mind.

Your job in de-escalating your friend is to cut through it all and find the core message of what is being said. Amazingly enough, this is easy to do once you know the trick. All you have to do is get out of your ego's way. You have an inherent, inborn capacity to understand precisely what another person is thinking, if you pay attention to that capacity. We mostly don't pay attention, focusing on our thoughts and feelings, and thus never realize these inherent powers.

Core messaging is largely a nonconscious process. By this, I mean that you will not be using a lot of cognitive effort or brain power to figure out what your friend really means. Instead, you will allow yourself to find the core message without thinking about it. It's a sort of unfocused focus that you develop. There are six steps that help you learn the process:

1. Listen and ignore the words.
2. Be in silence.
3. Wait for words or phrases to float into consciousness.
4. Allow a metaphor to come to mind.
5. Frame the core message using the metaphor.
6. Reflect back the core message.

Step One: Listen and Ignore the Words

Like affect labeling, you want to ignore the superficiality of the words being spoken. You are listening for meaning—"What is my friend really saying?"—not how she is saying it. Some ideas and words will strike you as important, but you don't have to worry about remembering them, as the idea will resonate with you. If you are paying attention to your friend's emotions too, you will find the gist, or general quality or essence, of what she is intending to convey.

Step Two: Be in Silence

Silence the chatter monkey inside you. Don't try to analyze anything. Just be in silence and wait. This is easy to do once you learn to relax and not worry about missing some crucial piece. You won't. Being in silence assures that you won't because parts of your brain are tracking what's going on and building a model of your friend's situation inside you.

Step Three: Wait for Words or Phrases to
Float into Consciousness

In a moment or so, some words or phrases will "float" into your conscious awareness. If you are patient and accepting, your powerful unconscious processing powers will find the best fit and bring them forward into your awareness. These are the ideas your brain has distilled from what your friend has been talking about. Your consciousness is way too slow and cumbersome to do this job effectively. Trust that the pattern and meaning-making parts of your brain that operate in the background will figure this out. In the beginning, your anxiety about whether something will come to you will slow you down. Once you experience it, however, you will see how effortless it is to wait.

Step Four: Allow a Metaphor to Come to Mind

Metaphors are linguistic devices used to convey ideas that might otherwise be hard to express. The role of metaphor is to provide a perspective from which to gain deeper understanding. In the case of core messaging, a metaphor will convey the essential meaning of what your friend is struggling to say in a deeply meaningful way. Try to find a metaphor that matches the ideas that materialized in your awareness. To help your creative brain think about some possibilities, you can break metaphors into groups.

Container metaphors use objects or examples of containment to express emotion. For example, you could say, "Anger is welling up inside you." Or, "You are filled with hope." Each of these metaphors evokes the idea of a container holding a feeling. You can modify the container so that it overflows: "Your frustration is boiling over." You can empty the container: "You are drained of energy."

Entity metaphors use machines or brittle objects to express emotion. "You feel like you are about to blow apart." "You are a nuclear plant on the verge of meltdown." Entity metaphors can act too: "You feel like you are being ground down to bits."

Substance metaphors use materials or qualities of materials to express emotion. "You are steaming mad." "You kept your cool while holding onto a raging fire inside you."

Core messages are best when they are framed as a metaphor. Unlike affect labeling, where you are naming the emotion, in core messaging you provide a concrete idea to capture an abstract and difficult to express emotional experience. For example, your friend might be expressing stress and pressure. The image of a steam boiler about to explode comes into your thoughts. That becomes your metaphor.

Step Five: Frame the Core Message Using the Metaphor

Using the metaphor as a guide, frame the core message. An easy way is to use a "You are" sentence. This should be simple and fast.

Step Six: Reflect Back the Core Message

The last step is to simply state what you believe the core message to be along with an affect label: "You are feeling like a boiler about to explode, and you are frustrated because you feel disrespected."

Usually, your friend will have several core messages. You will likely be spot on no matter which core message you tap into. Here's an example of how core messaging works:

Your Friend (F): "Mind if I tell you about something that is bothering me?"

You (Y): "Not at all. Pleased to listen."

F [taking a deep breath]: "Well, my son Robby comes home from college for the summer in a few weeks. We are pretty excited to have him visit. He is majoring in philosophy and sent us a lot of emails and photos when he was studying abroad in Paris. Maybe I should have a French dinner for him as a welcome-home treat. But I'm not a very good French cook. That new Whole Foods market might have some ideas about what to cook. I need to buy some nice wine anyway. I wonder when the parking situation there will get fixed. It's just a real issue getting in and out of that tight parking lot. Robby is coming home for a summer visit, and I am not sure how he will be, having been gone for two years overseas. The plumber is coming over to fix the guest-bathroom shower. It has been leaking and causing such a mess. Finally, we're doing something about it. Robby will stay in his old room, so he won't have to use that spare bath after all.

Y: "You are simmering with excitement at seeing Robby, and you are a little anxious about how he has changed since leaving home."

F: "Exactly."

This is a common occurrence. Your friend simply cannot articulate her excitement and anxiety. She flits from topic to topic, circling back and then flying off on another tangent. She intuitively knows that she is feeling something and does not have the presence of mind to sort through it all. Your core message cut right through the ramble to the issue that was driving her to distraction.

De-escalating Angry and Grieving Friends

Friendships are powerful social connections that often define our lives for decades. As we move through life with friends, we experience their triumphs and tragedies alongside them. Sometimes, the greatest expression of our friendship can be as an empathic listener. We aren't trying to fix anything, give advice, or commiserate. We are simply trying to be present in the moment to help a person close to us process a deep emotional experience. That is what friends are really for. The following sections will give you some new ideas about how to be with angry, grieving, upset friends in ways that will truly connect you both.

Listening to a Frustrated Friend

Here is another example of core messaging, with a frustrated friend:

Your Friend (F): "Mind if I tell you about something that is bothering me?"

You (Y): "Not at all. Pleased to listen."

F: "We have been having problems with Samantha, our sixteen-year-old. She is angry and disrespectful. We can't even have a decent conversation any more. At first, my husband wasn't that supportive, and I felt I was fighting a lonely battle, but he has become more supportive, and together we do try talking to her about her attitude. I have asked if she is having any difficulties, but she says she isn't. She has lots of nice friends and socializes a lot. I try to talk to her and show affection, but she pushes me away. I ask her to do things with me, but she always refuses. She has really been difficult, and it is making me feel very down. I feel almost bereaved, as if I have lost my daughter, because we used to be so close and do a lot together and laugh a lot. I don't know what to do. All I want is to have a relationship with her again. I love her so much."

Y: "You feel completely drained and empty and feel very lonely and unloved right now."

F: "Yeah. Thanks for listening."

Now try writing out a few different core messages that might be coming through in the conversation above. If you don't have the time to write out the core messages, think of what you might core message to your friend and say it out loud. Like affect labeling, until you get the core message right, you do not want to engage in any problem-solving. Remember the two-part basic formula:

1. First de-escalate.
2. Then problem-solve.

The unpracticed tendency is to give advice and problem-solve first. When you do this, you are soothing your anxieties at the expense of your friend. If you truly wish to be effective at calming your friend, you must learn to listen, core message, and affect label before you attempt any problem-solving. Since the entire process takes less than ninety seconds, I am sure you will master this skill quickly.

Listening to a Grief-Stricken Friend

Loss by death is an event no one wants to think about and is as inevitable as life. Despite this inevitability, we seem to be complete klutzes when close friends and relatives are grieving the death of a loved one. Many of us feel helpless, desperately wanting to help a grieving friend but confused as to how. There doesn't seem to be a Google Maps for navigating these deep emotional experiences. There are some services you can provide a grieving friend. One of them is to be a true listener. By now, you know that listening for your friend's emotions is the secret to helping that person through grief.

People in grief experience the full range of human emotions all at once. They feel lost, depressed, sad, angry, empty, and confused. When digesting an enormous loss, it can feel like no one else in the world understands. This can cause a bereaved person to push others away rather than accept the offered emotional support. Bear in mind that the grieving person is coming face-to-face with mortality, perhaps for the first time. While intellectually we all know that everything is impermanent, emotionally we hide from this reality. After a person loses a loved one, all relationships start to feel threatened. You realize that you can and will at some point lose everyone. This is a terrifying realization. Our psychological response is to shield ourselves from further pain and suffering of loss by pushing people away.

Clinical therapists are beginning to recognize that loss by death is traumatic and that symptoms of PTSD are common. The good news is that the grieving process, while intense, slowly resolves. My personal experience of loss, and my work as a peacemaker with families experiencing loss, suggests that the grieving process takes about eighteen months. However, the research literature suggests that the grieving process is highly variable.[11] No matter how long the process, we are resilient beings, and most people can come out of their grief to lead normal lives. The process, however, is awful and painful.

Affect labeling a grief-stricken friend requires your highest skill and compassion. If you are too heavy-handed, you will be seen as insensitive and uncaring. If you are too light, the calming effect will not take hold. Finding that balance is challenging. When artfully and sensitively executed, your affect labeling can be profoundly comforting to grieving friends.

Start with a specific question, not the generic "How are you doing?"

Here's one way it might go:

You (Y): "How's it been going the last couple of days?"
Your Friend (F): "It's okay. I'll survive."
Y: "You are really tired."
F: "Yeah. This has really been tough."
Y: "You have had to endure a lot of sadness."
F: "Uh-huh."
Y: "It's been overwhelming at times."
F: "Yeah. There are times when I can't do anything but sob."
Y: "Yeah. The grief is intense."
F: "And I am so tired after months of attending to my mother. It was a nightmare that never ended."
Y: "Tending to your mom's needs took a lot out of you."
F: "You have no idea."
Y: "No one can understand what you went through—it was so intense."

F: "And now I just miss her."

Y: "You feel alone and sad."

In this type of listening, you do not respond directly to what your friend is saying. Instead, you are using some paraphrasing, some core messaging, and some affect labeling. Your friend is processing her exhaustion and grief as you help her granulate her emotional experiences into something manageable for her. You continue in this vein as long as your friend keeps offering up new information and moves the conversation forward.

If she starts to repeat herself, she is blocking. Blocking occurs when someone cannot process consciously a set of emotions. She repeats herself over and over as she tries to make sense of what she is feeling. Your response is to affect label, even if you repeat yourself. Remember that you are providing the cognitive brain power that your friend lacks at the moment.

Keep your listening sessions short. Grieving friends are exhausted. Trying to do too much too fast will stretch them too far emotionally. Frequent, small encounters will be more welcomed than a few long ones.

When Not to Listen

As your new skills develop, you may have the disconcerting experience of friends wanting more of your time. Setting boundaries is, therefore, important. Just because you can calm someone down in ninety seconds does not mean that you have to. You are never obligated to listen to another person. There are times when you should not listen. They include:

- Your need to talk is greater than the other person's need to be listened to.
- You don't have time at the moment to listen.

- You are not in a good frame of mind to listen.
- You simply don't want to listen.
- You feel imposed upon.

Once you learn how to listen for emotions and core messages, you may see the world differently. Never be afraid to say no to anyone. Once you give yourself permission to say no, your ability to say yes will be more gentle and graceful. When you are able to listen, you will bestow a great gift on your speaker.

Listening to Insults and Disrespect

Friends and family get mad sometimes. They can be insulting and disrespectful to your face. How might you use your listening skills to handle these situations?

The biggest challenge is to keep your triggers under control. You will be angry. The question is how you will respond to your own upset. I have learned through direct experience that ignoring the insulting words and focusing on the speaker's emotions does wonders for keeping me grounded and centered. It's weird to think that your response to someone cussing you out is to reflect their feelings. However, once you have tried it, you will see that it is the fastest, most powerful way to stop an argument. One of the hidden benefits of listening is that you are shielded from insult. You will not even hear them.

Think about it. People who yell at you are angry and frustrated. They are experiencing strong emotions. Their emotions are directed at you, rightly or wrongly. You can choose to become escalated yourself, or you can choose to de-escalate the other person and find out what the real problem is.

Let's go through some insulting and provocative situations and see how you might respond.

Your Friend or Family Member (F): "Why don't you mind your own business? I am sick and tired of you butting into my stuff. Bug off!"

You (Y): "You are angry and frustrated and feel disrespected by me."

F: "Yeah!"

In this situation, the triggering words are personally insulting. Underneath, however, your friend is experiencing anger, frustration, and disrespect. Maybe you caused this or maybe not. However, getting back into your friend's face will not solve the problem. Your best strategy is to acknowledge and label your friend's emotions. As long as you ignore the words and focus only on your friend's feelings, you will protect yourself from being triggered.

F: "I hate you. Leave me alone. I don't want to talk to you."

Y: "You are really angry. You hate me. You are frustrated and feel abandoned."

F: "Yeah!"

If you listen to these words, they will be hurtful. You are being rejected by your friend, which is painful. However, if you focus on the emotions driving the words, you have an opportunity to calm your friend down and get to the root of the problem. Notice how direct you are in your response. The angrier the insult toward you, the more direct you have to be in your affect labeling. If your friend continues on his tirade, you hang with him.

When your friend finds that there is nothing to push against, he will tire and calm down because anger expends a lot of energy. It usually takes about forty-five seconds; that forty-five seconds may seem like forty-five years, however. You have to have the courage to stand the insults, no matter how hurtful. Remain focused on your friend's emotions. You can deal with your own reactive feelings later.

> F: "You never listen to me. I know you do not care about me. All you care about is yourself and how important you are."
> Y: "You feel disrespected and ignored. You are unloved and unappreciated."
> F: "Yeah!"

The class of insults involving "You don't care about me" generally means the opposite. Friends and family who say things like this in anger feel abandoned and unloved in the moment. Your strategy is to label those feelings so that your friend can process them. You know what will happen if you deny, excuse, or rationalize the emotions. Because you are invalidating your friend's feelings, you make matters worse.

> F: "What the heck were you thinking about? That was the dumbest, stupidest thing you have ever done! I can't believe you did that without talking to me first. Don't you know what this will do to us? How could you be so stupid? But I guess I shouldn't be surprised. You do stupid stunts like this all the time."
> Y: "You are angry, frustrated, and anxious. You are afraid. You feel alone and abandoned."
> F: "Yeah!"

Sometimes, we make costly mistakes. Before considering an apology and offer to make things right, de-escalate by affect labeling. When people are fired up about your mistakes, they are not ready for your apology. They have to be calm for an apology to have any meaning. Likewise, problem-solving to make things right can only happen when emotions are cooled down. Affect label first.

F: "F*ck you! I am not listening to your crap anymore!"

Y: "You are angry and don't feel heard. You feel completely disrespected."

F: "Yeah!"

Harsh language always indicates anger. After anger comes disrespect. Sometimes, there is a feeling of betrayal. Sometimes, there is underlying sadness and grief. You have to be willing to hang with your friend until she calms down.

F: "Shut up! I don't want any more of your sh*t!"

Y: "You are angry and feel deeply disrespected. You feel betrayed and ignored. You feel abandoned."

F: "Yeah!"

Frequently, emotions under insulting language between friends include sadness, grief, loneliness, and abandonment. Either due to fear of vulnerability or lack of awareness, upset friends do not easily express these deeper emotions. When you have the courage to affect label what is really going on, you help concretize the fundamental affects into consciousness where your friend can examine them and talk about them.

F: "You bastard! You lied to me. You SOB!"

Y: "You are angry and feel betrayed. You feel alone and abandoned."

F: "Yeah!"

As you read and internalize these difficult scenarios, you see the deep emotions over and over. Emotional repertoires are generally limited, and only a handful of basic emotions can be in play. Once you learn the code, the chaos goes away. You see deeply into your friends, understand their experiences, and have more compassion.

F: "I don't trust you. You lie and are unfaithful. I hate you!"

Y: "You are angry and feel betrayed. You feel alone and abandoned."

F: "Yeah!"

In any escalated situation with a friend, there are only three possible outcomes. First, the situation calms down, and you are able to problem-solve it to mutual satisfaction. Second, the situation calms down, and the relationship is ruptured, perhaps irrevocably. Third, the situation does not calm down, despite your best efforts. In that case, the only strategy left to you is to leave. Maybe the relationship will be reparable, maybe not. However, nothing positive can be done while your friend's emotions remain high. You allow time for a cooldown and then see what remains of your friendship.

Chapter Summary

In this chapter, we have learned:

- The six steps of core messaging:

    1. Listen and ignore the words.
    2. Be in silence.
    3. Wait for words or phrases to float into consciousness.
    4. Allow a metaphor to come to mind.
    5. Frame the core message using the metaphor.
    6. Reflect back the core message.

- How to listen to angry and grieving friends
- When not to listen
- How to listen to insults and disrespect

6

Peacemaking in Relationships

What strikes me as most remarkable about affect labeling is how it defuses the daily tensions in our relationship. When I am feeling insecure and say something not so pleasant, my husband does not react. He simply says, "Love, you are feeling insecure right now." When he does that, I somehow immediately calm down. Just knowing that he can feel my emotional experience and reflect it back to me rather than become defensive at my cutting remark is a huge reason why our relationship is so powerful and wonderful.

—**Aleya Dao**

This chapter is about our intimate relationships. In my view, arguments and fights in relationships are indications of deeper emotional experiences. The research shows that how you were raised emotionally as an infant and toddler has a direct link to the quality and satisfaction of your adult relationships.

Attachment theorists categorize infant and toddler attachments to their mothers as: secure, avoidant, or anxious. A secure attachment is just what it means—a baby feels safe and secure emotionally and physically. An avoidant attachment occurs when the baby experiences inconsistent emotional support from mother. In this relationship, the mother is sometimes close and loving and sometimes distant and unavailable. To cope with the stress of the inconsistency, the baby becomes avoidant of any attachment. An anxious attachment occurs when the baby is completely ignored emotionally. A baby's physical needs can be perfectly met, while his or her emotional needs are neglected. The baby forms an anxious attachment because the world is not emotionally safe for them.

In adulthood, the attachment of infancy translates directly into our intimate relationships. As in infancy, adult relationships cluster into the same three categories: secure, avoidant, and anxious. Adults comfortable with emotional closeness and able to depend on others (a more secure attachment style) have a higher sense of self-worth and greater social self-confidence and are more expressive. They tend to view people as trustworthy, dependable, and altruistic. They feel like they have control over their lives. These lucky people are less likely to have a love style characterized as game playing, obsessive, and overly logical, and more likely to have a style described as selfless.

Adults with a more anxious attachment style have negative beliefs about self and others. Greater anxiety in relationships is associated with a lower sense of self-worth, social self-confidence, and lack of assertiveness or sense of control. Adults who scored higher in anxiety were much more likely to have an obsessive, dependent love style.

Studies of heterosexual monogamous relationships show that women who are anxious in relationships have a deep fear of abandonment.[12] A woman's fear of abandonment is the strongest predictor of how a man sees the relationship. Men evaluate relationships much more negatively when their partner is anxious. Men are less satisfied with the relationship, report more conflict, feel less close to their partner, and are less likely to marry. Men also trust anxious partners less, have less faith, and view her as less predictable and dependable. Finally, men in these relationships rate the general level of communication as lower and say that they self-disclose less to their partner.

Women in relationships with men who are secure and able to maintain a close relationship report the relationship as very positive. Women feel closer to their partner, spend more free time with him, and experience less conflict in the relationship.

None of this should be particularly surprising. What this tells us, however, is how important the emotional experience of our partner is to the quality of the relationship. We tend to focus on our own emotional needs and pay less attention to what our partner is experiencing. This is, I believe, the source of fighting, arguments, and even violence in relationships. If we can learn to pay attention to the emotional experiences of our partners when they are stressed, anxious, tired, or triggered, we can prevent destructive and unhappy fighting. Ideally, it's a two-way street, such that your partner is attentive to your emotional experience. However, that may be asking a lot in the beginning. Let's start with what you can control.

De-escalating Intimate Relationships

You have the tools to be emotionally available in any of your personal relationships. You simply have to be willing to use them in uncomfortable moments when you are being challenged, accused, shamed, or blamed. As usual, your first defense against a flare up is to ignore the words.

The moment you start listening to the words, you are in danger of being triggered. As long as you focus on your partner's emotional experience in the moment, you are safe. You won't have the brain power to process and interpret the words.

When you understand the basic attachment schemes of secure, avoidant, and anxious, you see a common emotional pattern. Your partner becomes quite predictable. More important, you are able to calm down an angry, volatile moment quickly and compassionately. The layers of emotion that typically show up in relationship fights are:

Anger
Frustration
Disrespect
Being unheard
Anxiety
Fear
Sadness
Abandonment

Your partner generally starts at anger and cycles down to anxiety. Fear, sadness, and abandonment are often present, but your partner may be unaware of them. You can go there if you sense it appropriate and safe to do so.

In the beginning, you want to use one affect label at a time and make the label almost a conversational throwaway. You are testing the waters to see if affect labeling has an effect on your partner, and you are reducing your own emotional risk of failure. Keep it simple and short until you have built up confidence in the skill.

We first look at several common arguments and scenarios where a woman is listening to her boyfriend's or husband's emotions. Then we look at scenarios where a man is listening to his girlfriend's or wife's emotions. In each set of examples, the person is being accused, attacked, blamed, or dismissed or is facing passive-aggressive behavior. Keep your cool and imagine yourself in the situation.

Listening to a Man's Emotions

Your Boyfriend or Husband (B/H): "Would you stop that damn texting and pay attention to me for once?"

You (Y): "You're frustrated."

B/H: "Yeah. Every time we go out to dinner, you pull out your phone and start texting your friends. It pisses me off."

Y: "You're angry and frustrated and feel disrespected."

B/H: "Damn right I do. It's bullsh*t."

Y: "You don't feel loved or appreciated. You feel invisible and unworthy."

B/H: "Yeah."

Instead of bristling up your defenses and lashing back, you made the effort to focus on his emotional experience. Notice that you did not add anything to the labels. In other words, you did not add in any context such as "You are angry and frustrated *that I am texting right now.*" The reason that you don't add the context (in italics) is because your texting may not be the root cause of the anger and frustration. Your texting may only be the triggering event based on stuff that happened earlier in the day that has nothing to do with your texting. Keep your affect labeling simple, simple, simple. This is harder than it seems. Practice will make it obvious to you.

B/H: "I just wanted to watch the damn game."

Y: "You are frustrated."

B/H: "Yeah. I am frustrated. Every time I want to watch a football game, you find a way to stop me. I'm sick and tired of it."

Y: "You don't feel respected."

B/H: "Yeah. You crowd in on me sometimes."

Y: "You feel a little anxious and nervous."

B/H: "I do. I don't like feeling smothered."

Y: "You don't like feeling smothered, and you feel sadness at not being truly loved."

B/H: "Yeah. How did you know?"

This was a bit more of a stretch. Guys who feel smothered are avoidant. They grew up in emotionally cold and rejecting families and never learned how to attach to another. Yet they still have the innate drive to love and be loved. They are caught in a horrible dilemma of which they are generally unaware. When you try to get emotionally closer, they start to panic. This is reported as smothering, and the emotions are anxiety and fear. Underneath it all is the feeling of abandonment and being unloved. This is a very common pattern and the cause of many arguments and fights in relationships. You have the ability to stop this cycle by validating his emotions through affect labeling. If you keep your statements short and simple, you are less likely to get pushback.

B/H: "Jeez, you borrowed my car and left the tank empty again. I ran out of gas before I could make it to a gas station."

Y: "You are angry and frustrated."

B/H: "Damn right I am. I can't depend on you."

Y: "You feel disrespected."

B/H: "Of course I do. Wouldn't you be pissed off if I left your car with an empty tank?"

Y: "You feel unappreciated, alone, and unsupported."

B/H: "Damn right I do."

Y: "You feel unloved and abandoned."

B/H: "Yes! Exactly."

An empty gas tank is an annoyance, at best. It is not worth fighting about. However, your guy has an avoidant attachment mechanism going on. He can't trust anyone, can't depend on anyone, and has isolated himself emotionally. The empty gas tank is not the issue. The issue is his feeling of abandonment that was triggered by this situation. Your best response is not to fight back and defend yourself. That will only increase his feeling of isolation and reinforce his avoidance strategies. Instead, like a jujitsu master, you go to the heart of the matter by affect labeling.

As his feelings are acknowledged and validated, he calms down. You demonstrate that you are dependable, reliable, and present for him, unlike his parents. Over time, he might shift. There are no guarantees here. However, this is the only way your relationship with him has a chance of working into something healthy and happy.

B/H: "Why do you keep bringing up Monica? That was three years ago, and it was completely innocent. Why can't you just let it drop?"

Y: "You are angry and frustrated."

B/H: "Yes, I am. I am tired of you shaming me."

Y: "You feel unappreciated and disrespected."

B/H: "Of course I do. You keep bringing up Monica to pull my chain. It pisses me off."

Y: "You are pissed off and you are sad."

B/H: "Yes. I just want to be loved."

Y: "You feel unloved and abandoned."

B/H: "I do."

You started this one, probably unconsciously. You might have been feeling isolated or alone. By pulling his trigger, you got a reaction that would normally lead to a fight. This time, you tried something different. By following his emotions, you validated that he is hurt by your accusation. You calmed him down, created a small safe place for him to be in his emotions, and stopped the usual fight. This is a big shift for both of you.

B/H: "You told me to be ready to go twenty-five minutes ago, and I dropped what I was doing. Here we are, and you haven't even taken a shower yet. We are going to be so late. What is wrong with you?"

Y: "You are frustrated and feel disrespected."

B/H: "Yes. You do this all the time. I try to honor your time. Why can't you honor mine?"

Y: "You feel unappreciated and unsupported."

B/H: "I would really like you to be prompt and ready to go when you say you will be."

Y: "You are anxious and don't feel in control."

B/H: "Yes. We made a commitment to be at the restaurant to see our friends."

Y: "You feel shame and some sadness."

B/H: "Yes."

Being late to a dinner outing may be a faux pas and discomfiting. However, the underlying issue is not about that. It is about respect and shame. Your guy doesn't feel in control when you are running late. He also feels responsible for the two of you and anticipates feeling the shame of not fulfilling a commitment to friends. He might fall into the anxious attachment category, where control, order, and predictability are important. By acknowledging his emotions without arguing back, you have given him the opportunity to unpack a little of this. He calms down, and you can problem-solve appropriately.

> **B/H**: "I am really tired of you accusing me of flirting with other girls. It's really pissing me off."
> **Y**: "You are frustrated."
> **B/H**: "Yes. No matter what I do, I can't seem to convince you of my loyalty to you."
> **Y**: "You feel unappreciated and unsupported."
> **B/H**: "Yes. When will you stop this jealousy crap?"
> **Y**: "You feel disrespected and shamed."
> **B/H**: "I do. You are constantly accusing me of infidelity. It's driving me nuts."
> **Y**: "You feel unloved and abandoned."
> **B/H**: "Yep."

Undeserved jealousy is difficult for both you and your guy. You can let your own insecurities lead to fights and arguments, or you can validate his emotions. You need your feelings acknowledged too, but right now he's the one who is escalated. By affect labeling, you calm him down, and you both appreciate the pain of jealous accusations.

You might notice that under the "You" dialogue the listening responses are similar in the previous different scenarios. What you are learning is that the human emotional repertoire can really be simplified to just a few emotions. You will discover that your partner repeatedly cycles through the same emotions in a very predictable way.

You have the formula now. Write out the conversation that started your last argument, just like the scenarios. In the "You" column, write out the emotions he experienced as if you were affect labeling him. Write out his probable responses and continue until you get to the bottom of his emotional experience. This is good practice and will make affect labeling real for you.

Listening to a Woman's Emotions

Time to flip to the other side. In the scenarios that follow, I have created common situations that guys face with their girlfriends or wives. Usually, these situations resolve in arguments or stony silence. As you will see, by affect labeling, you may be able to turn the situation into something more positive and peaceful.

As with the first set of scenarios, you as the guy have done or said something that has triggered your girlfriend or wife. Your mission, should you decide to accept it, is to de-escalate her in ninety seconds or less. Problem-solving generally follows.

Your Girlfriend or Wife (G/W): "I deserve someone who gives a sh*t, and you don't."

You (Y): "You are angry and frustrated."

G/W: "You never show up, never help out, and lie around all day while I work my butt off."

Y: "You feel disrespected and unappreciated."

G/W: "All you do is watch your stupid sports or play your games."

Y: "You feel unsupported and unloved."

G/W: "That's right. And so would you if you had to put up with what I do."

Y: "You feel alone and abandoned."

G/W: "Yes. I do."

The formula remains the same: ignore the words and reflect the emotions. This is probably a good point to talk about your tone of voice. Obviously, you have to sincerely want to affect label and calm down your girlfriend or wife. If you try to use affect labeling to manipulate, it may backfire on you. The tone of your voice should be appropriate to the situation. If she is yelling, you want to use an initial tone of voice that is loud, but not as loud. If you pitch your voice under hers, she begins to quiet down and become more reflective. As her volume decreases, follow her down and stay quieter than her. You are essentially matching her emotional intensity at its peak and in its decline with your pitch and volume.

> **G/W**: "If you were a real man, you would get out and make something of yourself instead of making excuses why you are a failure."
> **Y**: "You are angry."
> **G/W**: "I'm tired of being around a failure."
> **Y**: "You are frustrated and sad."
> **G/W**: "I just wish you would back to school or get a job. I don't want to be stuck in this dead end for the rest of my life."
> **Y**: "You are unhappy and anxious."
> **G/W**: "I'm really frustrated."
> **Y**: "You are really frustrated."

This is another classic fight-brewing provocation. You can get mad and defensive, or you can de-escalate and problem-solve. It doesn't matter whether you are a lazy, unmotivated, apathetic guy in this moment. Nor does it matter if she is completely wrong and you are an ass-kicking entrepreneur. What matters is her emotional experience and how you choose to respond to it. Insults hurt, but fighting back only makes things worse. You are better off if you ignore the words and reflect the feelings. You can talk things over once she is calm. You will never convince her out of her beliefs in this moment.

> **G/W**: "I can't even talk to you right now I'm so pissed."
> **Y**: "You are pissed off."
> **G/W**: "Yeah."

Y: "Pissed off and really frustrated."

G/W: "Yeah."

Sometimes, short and sweet is all you can do. If your girlfriend or wife is truly pissed at you, a little bit of affect labeling is all you can get away with. Even then, a little bit goes a long way toward peace. If she seems open to talking more after this initial reflection, keep at it. Guess at the underlying emotions. Although anger presented first and most intensely, there are other emotions underneath that are really driving her reality. Your job, if she lets you, is to help her sort them out.

G/W: "I'm fine."

Y: "You are royally pissed off."

G/W: "No, I'm not."

Y: "You are frustrated as hell and feel disrespected."

G/W: "Damn right."

The classic "I'm fine" statement when the tone of voice and body language convey the opposite is an avoidant behavior. She is not fine, but in this moment she does not feel safe enough to share. She denies her own reality to avoid confronting her emotions and you. If you make sharing safe by affect labeling, she is likely to open up and talk more. You have to want that to happen. If you don't, then don't affect label her. Affect labeling creates a deeper intimacy for a few seconds as each of you experiences her emotions. You are both vulnerable, and that may be scary. No one ever said the path of peace was easy. You have to have a lot of courage to overcome your own fears, self-doubts, and anxieties.

G/W: "Do you think I look fat in these jeans?"

Y: "You are feeling really anxious about your weight right now."

G/W: "Yeah."

Y: "You are feeling insecure and unloved."

G/W: "Yeah."

Y: "You are afraid of being abandoned and alone."

G/W: "Yeah."

Y: "And right now, you don't feel like anyone loves you."

G/W: "Yeah."

Normally, if she asks, "Do I look fat in these jeans?" you know you are facing a no-win situation. Any answer is a bad one. If you say yes, you are screwed. If you say no, she won't believe you and think you are lying to placate her. The strategy for dealing with this situation is to remember what is driving the question. It's not about her appearance; it's about her feeling insecure in the moment. Her insecurity will pass one way or the other. You can help her deal with it by affect labeling it out to help her uncover the real feelings.

These scenarios show you how simple it is to de-escalate if you are willing to ignore the words and pay attention to the emotions. There is no need to fight, argue, get defensive, or engage in destructive behaviors in your relationships. You might face a little resistance from time to time, and that is normal. Just back off and try again in ten minutes.

A Word on Dating

Affect labeling builds a sense of shared intimacy very quickly. Early in dating, before there's even a relationship, you may use affect labeling to powerful effect. Your date will respond very positively toward you as you listen in a way he or she has perhaps never before experienced on a first or second date.

I was teaching affect labeling at Southern Methodist University. I gave out the assignment to affect label a stranger at Starbucks. The next morning, I asked for stories. One of my students, a young woman, raised her hand.

"What happened?" I asked.

"Well, I went to Starbucks early this morning. While I was in a pretty long line, a guy behind me dropped a bunch of papers on the floor. I bent over and started scooping them up for him. As I handed him his papers, I said, 'You are embarrassed.' He lit up, saying, 'Yeah.' Then he started hitting on me!"

We all laughed. She had just learned that even a little affect labeling makes you very attractive. The moral of the story is don't affect label indiscriminately. You may or may not like the attention it will generate.

Listening and Problem-Solving with Your Partner

Marriage and long-term committed relationships follow an individual's typical life arc, with new twists. Now the task is living lives together. This includes weaving two financial worlds, social worlds, work worlds, and family worlds together. Child bearing and rearing become important. Making money and perhaps advancing in careers take up time. Stress becomes common as we try to balance these new tasks. The opportunity for conflict, arguments, and fights grows with the added responsibilities, the perceived loss of autonomy and freedom, and the tensions of everyday life.

Added to all of this is the sad fact that, in the busyness of life, our emotional needs may go unmet. And our spouse's emotional needs are often neglected as well. This leads to loneliness within the relationship, sadness, and deep grief that is vaguely felt and certainly not expressed. There does not seem to be time for vulnerability, and emotional trust withers.

Many couples cope with this by focusing on their children. The children give back love, which is intoxicating and masks the emotional desert that the couple is traversing. When the children are nonloving because they are in their emotional experience, the parental reaction can be based on a deep sense of rejection and hurt, causing parents to lash out at their children. Thus, the children learn not to be aware of their emotions, and the cycle repeats. If the parents never learned the skills of emotional competency, they may be carrying all of the programming from their parents and grandparents. That programming is passed on unconsciously to the children.

In this life, conflict is inevitable. Arguments and fights result. Hurt, resentment, anger, and frustration grow. Of course, all of this adds to the stress of surviving in modern life. It's not always very "happily ever after."

It doesn't have to be this way.

Learning and using the listening and problem-solving skills presented here can help break this cycle. As a testimonial to the power of this work, my wife, Aleya Dao, and I are blissfully married. We have some conflict from time to time and some stress, just like everyone else. We choose to respond in those moments by focusing on each other's emotional experience and affect labeling. Works like a charm.

By now, you know the drill:

- Ignore the words.
- Guess at the emotions.
- Reflect back the emotions with a simple declaration.
- Use "You" statements, not "I" statements.
- Don't ask questions.
- Stop after ninety seconds or when you see the relaxation response, whichever comes first.

With your spouse or partner, who has never been exposed to this level of listening, you modify the basic pattern. Ideally, your affect labeling should be undetectable by your spouse the first time you try it. If your spouse catches you, you are likely to receive pushback. The classic response is something like "What are you doing? Don't do that stuff to me!"

You might be tempted to give up. Don't. This skill takes practice, and practice takes time. Failure is inevitable, and failure is the only path to mastery. You have my permission to fall flat on your face with this, as long as you don't quit. Forgive yourself the error and pump yourself up by reassuring yourself that you are learning how to serve others.

To keep the risk of failure low until you build confidence, follow these modified rules:

1. Don't affect label the first time in highly escalated situations.
2. Keep your reflection limited to one emotion: "You are angry."
3. Keep your tone of voice casual and conversational, if appropriate. Make sure you do not sound patronizing or disrespectful.
4. Observe your spouse's response. If it's good, try again. If it's bad, back off and try later.

One trick that might be of real use to you is to pick a positive situation to affect label. Here's a scenario that shows how that might play out in a couple of seconds.

> **Your Spouse (S):** "Touchdown! Yeah! Did you see that? That was amazing!"
> **You (Y):** "That was amazing. You're really excited."
> **S:** "Huh? Yeah, that got my blood going. Fantastic!"

You pick a pretty low-risk condition with an exciting moment. You make a quick reflection as part of your reaction to the touchdown. Your spouse is confused because you've never done that before. However, because the moment passes by, your spouse refocuses on the game. This is a great start. Don't try affect labeling again during the game or even again that day. Let it be. You have done enough.

Let's say that you get caught. How do you gracefully back out when your spouse pushes back? Here's a scenario that might give you some ideas:

S: "Touchdown! Yeah! Did you see that? That was amazing!"

Y: "That was amazing. You're really excited."

S: "What? How can you know what I'm feeling? What psycho-babble are you learning now?"

Y: "Didn't mean to upset or offend you. I just saw that you were excited about the touchdown and commented on it."

S: "Huh! Well, I don't like you doing that peacemaking crap on me."

Y: "Okay, sorry to have upset you."

Usually, if you apologize and back off, the matter is forgotten. If your spouse wants to pick a fight about it, you can simply offer up that you are trying to listen in a deeper way.

S: "Touchdown! Yeah! Did you see that? That was amazing!"

Y: "That was amazing. You're really excited."

S: "What? How can you know what I'm feeling? What psycho-babble are you learning now?"

Y: "Didn't mean to upset or offend you. I just saw that you were excited about the touchdown and commented on it."

S: "Huh! Well, I don't like you doing that peacemaking crap on me."

Y: "Okay, sorry to have upset you."

S: "Well, it bugs me when you try that stuff on me."

Y: "Well, I was trying to listen to you at a deeper level. I want you to feel heard and understood."

S: "Hmph!"

What is this telling you? Remember that most people, including your spouse, are emotionally incompetent. An early-twentieth-century philosopher, Thorstein Veblen, coined the term *trained incapacity*. That's what we have in our relationships: a trained incapacity to listen to each other at a deep level. That incapacity was programmed into us by our parents, our peers, and our culture. Emotions are bad; rationality is good. Mr. Spock is admirable.

The result of this incapacity is that your spouse experiences anxiety. At an unconscious level, the brain experiences a new and unrecognizable social cue, your affect label. Since your spouse's brain (and yours and mine) cannot distinguish between a physical threat and a social threat, this new stimulus is categorized as, at best, suspicious, and probably dangerous. This judgment occurs outside your spouse's consciousness, is nearly instantaneous, and results in immediate, knee-jerk defensive behavior.

Your spouse's resistance doesn't mean you failed; it means that you succeeded too well. You truly did touch your spouse's emotional centers in a new way. Your spouse is not quite ready for what is coming in your relationship. Your tactic is to back off and try again later. Next time, see if you can affect label without setting off the fire alarms. Just be more subtle. It will work. You will see.

Let's look at a scenario where it works perfectly:

S: "Touchdown! Yeah! Did you see that?"

Y: "That was amazing. You're really excited."

S: "Yeah, I am. Did you see that pass? Incredible. And the catch in all of that coverage?"

Y: "You are surprised and pleased and impressed with that."

S: "I am. You know, that's the first time you have ever taken an interest in football. Usually, you just tolerate it."

Y: "You are surprised and happy."

S: "Yep. I feel like you really get it. Thanks."

Something happens here that is common too. The spouse says, "You know, that's the first time you have ever taken an interest in football." The spouse doesn't consciously connect your affect labeling with emotions. Instead, there is a symbolic transfer of meaning from being listened to emotionally to taking an interest in football. This happens a lot when people cannot articulate their emotions. Instead of struggling, the unconscious brain selects something easier to grasp, like football, and creates meaning around it. Cognitive psychologists call this the *substitution effect*. Once you see it, you will see it often.

Let's look at some other common scenarios. Here's one that you might recognize:

S: "Work today was hell."

Y: "You are frustrated."

S: "Yeah, those jerks in sales always overpromise to the customer and then expect us to bail them out."

Y: "You feel disrespected and unappreciated."

S: "Yeah. And they always want the bailout at the last minute, so we have to disrupt our work flow."

Y: "You are angry and anxious because you can't coordinate your work flow."

S: "Yeah. Our bonuses are tied to production, and when these bozos screw us up, we are really stressed. It's like we are saving their bonuses at the expense of ours."

Y: "You feel that the situation is unfair."

S: "Damn right. Thanks for listening. I didn't mean to unload on you like that."

This is a classic use of affect labeling and maybe a little core messaging to help your spouse work through the emotions of a difficult day. You see the relaxation response as you touch on the core emotions. This is a good place to point out the difference between sympathy and empathy. When you affect label, you are being empathetic. If you are just listening and providing appropriate attending and following cues, you are being sympathetic. Here's the same conversation with sympathy instead of empathy:

S: "Work today was hell."

Y: "Hmmm. Sorry you had such a bad day."

S: "Yeah, those jerks in sales always overpromise to the customer and then expect us to bail them out."

Y: "Yeah, I know what you mean."

S: "Yeah. And they always want the bailout at the last minute, so we have to disrupt our work flow."

Y: "They are jerks to do that to you."

S: "Yeah. Our bonuses are tied to production, and when these bozos screw us up, we are really stressed. It's like we are saving their bonuses at the expense of ours."

Y: "Wow!"

S: "Oh well, nothing to do for it. I need a drink."

There's nothing wrong with the sympathetic response. However, if you really want to bring someone down to calmness from emotional upset, you have to be empathetic. The only sure way to do that is through affect labeling.

Defusing Arguments and Fights

The acid test of all of this is defusing an argument or fight with your spouse. Let's start by setting the bar of success very low. If you can stop one argument out of ten from exploding, you are doing great work. In learning new ways of being, we tend to expect too much of ourselves. In this case, be satisfied with incremental progress. (But I think you will do a lot better than that.)

Here's a scenario where your spouse is trying to escalate the conflict with insults:

S: "You always do this. You always do this."

Y: "You are frustrated and angry."

S: "Why do you always do this to me?"

Y: "You feel disrespected."

S: "Just for once in your life, listen to me."

Y: "You don't feel heard. You are really anxious and afraid."

S: "You never listen to me."

Y: "You are sad and feel invisible. You don't feel heard, and that makes you feel lonely and unloved."

S: "Yeah."

The secret is recognizing the blocking. Blocking is when your spouse repeats the same thing over and over again. Here, the blocking state is around listening. Your spouse doesn't register your first affect label attempt. Instead, the old programing kicks in. Your spouse is not expecting to be listened to, so the first insult comes out: "Just for once in your life, listen to me," followed by, "You never listen to me."

When you see blocking, you know that there is a deeper emotional experience that your spouse can't talk about. Typically, your spouse does not have the emotional granularity to express himself or herself. The response is to accuse you of not listening. Somehow, you are expected to figure out your spouse's feelings and get them. Well, with affect labeling, you do just that. In this case, by guessing at the sadness, the sense of being invisible and being unloved, you are able to get to the root of the feelings. The argument ends.

Sometimes, money ignites arguments. Here's a common scenario and how to handle it:

S: "Where did you go to lunch today?"
Y: "We did Italian."
S: "What'd you have?"
Y: "Chicken Caesar salad."
S: "How much did you spend?"
Y: "Thirteen bucks."
S: "Thirteen bucks! On a stupid salad. We can't afford that!"

Substitute the salad and the thirteen bucks for anything else. Usually, with this kind of fight, you defend your autonomy and resist the implication that you are wasting the family treasure. The deeper insinuation is that you don't love your spouse, which inflames the argument.

Try it this way and watch what happens:

S: "Where did you go to lunch today?"
Y: "We did Italian."
S: "What'd you have?"
Y: "Chicken Caesar salad."
S: "How much did you spend?"
Y: "Thirteen bucks."
S: "Thirteen bucks! On a stupid salad. We can't afford that!"
Y: "You are angry."
S: "Yeah, I'm angry. We can't afford that kind of money on what we make."
Y: "You are anxious and frustrated."
S: "Yes. We have rent to pay and we buy groceries, and you go off and spend thirteen bucks on a fancy Italian salad."
Y: "You are sad and feel abandoned. You don't feel supported."
S: "Yeah."

You might be surprised at how many times the argument is really not about the money. Money becomes a symbol for other things, like love, appreciation, support, and emotional safety. Criticizing spending money becomes a convenient shorthand for saying, "I'm worried about our survival," or, "I don't feel safe," or, "I am unloved." If you can ignore the words about money and spending to focus on the real emotions, you can cut through to your spouse's true feelings and validate them. Then you can problem-solve, if money is a real issue.

Here is a difficult scenario. The issue is about when to start a family. It has been the source of intense arguments.

> **You (Y):** "You have to get control of your anger."
> **Your spouse (S)** [sarcastically]: "Oh, we have to get my anger under control because I am the problem."
> **Y:** "We have to come to grips with the fact that even the smallest discussion erupts into a huge fight."
> **S:** "It's because of your failure to commit to having a family. You can't commit to that."

In the usual course, this conversation escalates quickly to shouting at each other. In one instance, if you are the husband, you are shut down by your wife's relentless attacks. She is enormously frustrated and hurt that her desire for children is being thwarted. You are scared to death of bringing a child into the world with a wife who is so explosive.

Here's one way it might work out:

> **Y:** "You have to get control of your anger."
> **W** [sarcastically]: "Oh, we have to get my anger under control because I am the problem."
> **Y:** "We have to come to grips with the fact that even the smallest discussion erupts into a huge fight."
> **W** [with rising, angry voice]: "It's because of your failure to commit to having a family. You can't commit to that."

Y: "You are frustrated and angry."

W: "Yes. Beyond frustrated and angry."

Y: "You feel ignored and disrespected."

W: "Yes!"

Y: "You are anxious and confused and don't know what to expect."

W: "Yes!"

Y: "You are sad and lonely. You feel abandoned and unloved."

W [starting to cry]: "Yes!"

At least this time around, the fight does not escalate and end in angry withdrawal. There are serious issues in play here that may need the help of a marriage and family counselor. However, by affect labeling, you have taken the first step in moving away from the never-ending cycle of argument and rejection.

How to Get the Other Person to Listen

By now, if you have been practicing these ideas, you may be wondering how you get listened to. It's great to be able to de-escalate an angry kid, friend, or spouse, but what happens when you need to be listened to?

There is no easy answer. Now that you know what real, deep empathic listening is all about, you won't be satisfied with the same-old, same-old. One idea is to find a trusted friend, give her a copy of this book, and work through the chapters together. Then, she can practice her skills on you, and you can be listened to.

If you have a partner or spouse who is open to learning, you can try the same thing. However, it can be more challenging because of the intimacy or lack of intimacy between you. Lots of emotions can come up in practice that may lead you into scary places. As long as you both have the courage to face your demons, this work can be effective and rewarding. If you start affect labeling your kids, you will find them naturally affect labeling in a matter of days. Don't be surprised if they start to affect label you. Accept the gift they are giving you with grace.

Another way to ease a partner or family member into affect labeling is through the peace circle process I introduced in chapter 4. Since you have to earn your turn to speak in the circle, it is a safe and low-risk space to learn how to listen to another person's emotions.

De-escalating After Divorce

I was stuck. The couple was screaming at each other. As a mediator, I felt helpless to stop the arguing. The dispute was trivial, at first impression. Twenty years ago, when this couple had been married, there had been an automobile accident involving the kids. The settlement required a minor's trust, which meant that the $18,000 from the insurance company could not be spent without a court order.

After the divorce, the ex-husband failed to make spousal support payments, and the ex-wife came on hard times. She talked to her adult kids about the money in the trust. The kids told her, "Mom, do not worry about it. Take the money and use it any way you need to." So, she did.

The ex-husband found out and was furious. He filed a lawsuit against her for breach of fiduciary duty and contempt of court. By the time they made it to me, they had spent more than $50,000 in attorneys' fees over an $18,000 problem.

As I sat there listening to them insult each other in loud voices, suddenly, an idea occurred to me.

"Stop!" I demanded. They both looked at me. Fortunately, they stopped yelling. "Let us try something different. Viv, I want you to listen to Michael and ignore his words. Can you do that?"

"What do you mean, ignore his words?" she asked.

"I want you to ignore his words and tell us what you think he is feeling as he tells his story. Can you do that?" I said.

"I do not know," she responded.

"Are you willing to try?" I asked.

"I guess so," she said carefully.

"Good. Let us give it a try," I said. "Michael, try telling your story again."

Michael started telling his story. After about five seconds, Viv exclaimed, "You lying bastard. All you do is lie."

"Whoa!" I exclaimed. "Viv, see if you can ignore his words and just pay attention to what he is feeling. What do you think he is feeling right now?"

"I do not know," she said.

"Okay. Let us try again," I said. "Michael, again, please."

Michael started again, and before Viv could erupt, I stopped him and turned to her.

"Viv, what do you think Michael is feeling right now?"

Viv paused. "Well, he is really angry."

"Great. Tell him that," I said.

Viv looked at Michael and said, "You are really angry."

"Perfect," I said.

"Damn right I am angry. I am really pissed and frustrated. All you do is disrespect me and the kids and do what you want to do," Michael exclaimed.

I could see Viv starting to bristle. "Viv, ignore his words. What is he feeling?"

"Ah, he's feeling frustrated and disrespected," she said.

"Beautiful," I said. "Keep going."

Michael continued with his story. I would let him go a sentence or two, especially when he said something inflammatory and disrespectful. Then I stopped him and had Viv reflect to him what his feelings were. We continued like this for ten minutes until Michael finished his story.

After he finished, I turned to Viv and asked, "What was that like?"

"Really empowering. I did not get angry at all, once I started paying attention only to his feelings and ignoring the words," she said.

I looked at Michael. By now, he had his face in his hands and was quietly sobbing. This was pretty surprising.

"Michael, are you okay?" I asked.

Michael composed himself and looked up at Viv. He said, "That is the first time that you have listened to me in twenty-five years." She was dumbfounded, and so was I.

I had Viv tell her story. I told Michael to ignore the words and pay attention to Viv's feelings. Initially, he had the same problem that Viv did in wanting to spin what he heard. But like Viv, he quickly learned to ignore the words and pay attention only to the emotions.

When the storytelling was done, Michael said, "This whole thing is really stupid. I am sorry I filed the lawsuit. I was just really hurt that you did not consult me. Let's just call it quits."

And with that, a lawsuit that had been extremely bitter and expensive for two people who were formerly married to each other ended. I was floored.

What had just happened?

I did not have a clue but was happy that these nice people were able to get this problem behind them, and that I was able to help them. I pretty much forgot about what I had done for a couple of years. At the time, I didn't know that I had stumbled across affect labeling. It wasn't until I came across Matthew Lieberman's 2007 brain scanning study that I realized the significance of what had happened between Viv and Michael.

As I mentioned in chapter 1, Lieberman and his colleagues at UCLA provided important research behind this book's de-escalation process. And what I discovered was that affect labeling decreased activity in the emotional centers of the brain (diminished response in the amygdala and other limbic areas) and increased activity in executive function centers of the brain (right ventrolateral prefrontal cortex). As executive function increased with affect labeling, emotional reactivity decreased. In short, affect labeling was shown to de-escalate emotions along a distinct neural pathway. This was the empirical proof that affect labeling was not some esoteric, touchy-feely thing but a true technique based on hard science. And that's when I began to refine the idea, develop skills, test them, and deploy them in my mediations, workshops, and academic courses.[13]

Co-Parenting

You may be divorced from your spouse, but you are co-parents forever. Co-parenting children as ex-spouses is one of the more difficult challenges of life. When it comes to making decisions about children, divorced parents have to want to find a middle ground. If you and your ex are not in a place where you can negotiate, compromise, and extend some reasonable cooperation to each other, you and the kids are in for a world of hurt. If the conflict between you and your ex is such that there is a reflexive, unthinking rejection of what the other parent has to say, then you and your children suffer.

There are two levels of pain that deprive people of the ability to work together as co-parents. Parents at the first level of pain honestly believe that the children should have a healthy relationship with the other parent. Their problem is that they cannot control their frustration, bitterness, or hurt. When their painful feelings are triggered, they lash out against the targeted parent. After regaining control, they usually feel guilty about what they did and back off from their bad behaviors. They mean well, but will lose control because the intensity of their feelings overwhelms them.

If both parents are suffering at this first level of pain, the co-parenting is very difficult. However, if one can reach out to affect label and problem-solve, the other parent will respond. It takes huge courage and patience to work through the emotional dysfunction, anger, and mistrust. Over time, however, the co-parenting relationship can be improved.

The second level of pain is much more difficult. A divorced parent at this level of pain feels intense anger, abandonment, and betrayal. These strong feelings don't heal. Instead, the feelings intensify by a forced co-parenting relationship with a person they despise. Just having to see or talk to the other parent triggers the hate. They are trapped in a hell of anger that they cannot escape. If the feelings are mutual, every argument will end up in a custody or visitation battle in front of a judge. These parents are obsessed with destroying the children's relationship with the targeted parent. Their beliefs sometimes become delusional and irrational. No one, especially the court, can convince them that they are wrong. Anyone who tries is the enemy.

The battle becomes "us against them." They have an unquenchable anger because they believe that they have been victimized by the targeted parent. Whatever they do to protect the children is justified. They have a desire for vengeance and seek to punish the other parent with court orders that would interfere or block the targeted parent from seeing the children. The court's authority does not intimidate them. They often believe in a higher cause, protecting the children at all cost. This parent is extraordinarily difficult to work with as a co-parent. However, with some knowledge of what is going on, there are strategies that may help. Let us start with the six needs of victims.

The Six Needs of Victims

As a mediator, I have seen the cycle of victimization play out over and over again. In many conflicts, both sides feel victimized. They are trapped, allowing themselves to be disempowered by the other. Many years ago, I attended a lecture by my friend and colleague Erica Ariel Fox. She talked about the six needs of victims. The needs are:

- Vengeance
- Vindication
- Validation
- Being heard
- Creating meaning
- Safety

Vengeance

The need for vengeance is powerful because it is based upon the reward centers of the brain. Vengeance, unlike many other emotions and affects, is anticipatory. We reward ourselves with little squirts of dopamine when we imagine punishing our tormentor. Dopamine is the neurochemical associated with pleasure and learning. Dopamine circuits are why cocaine and heroin are so addicting. Those drugs mimic the effects of dopamine.

Because of our anticipation of righteous judgment against our enemy, we are spurred to action. The problem is this: if we are able to exact vengeance, we get no dopamine release. We receive very little brain candy for thumping the other guy. The effect is to feel depressed, let down, angry, and unfulfilled. We hold this belief about how good we will feel in righting the huge injustice done to us, and when retribution is exacted, we feel absolutely nothing. Even though justice has been meted out, we feel as if it has not. I saw this effect play out over and over again in my trial lawyer days. I represented too many clients who, after winning at trial, remained disappointed and angry at the outcome even though it was a legal victory. The win did not give them the release they were expecting. This was one of the main reasons I left the courtroom to become a peacemaker.

Vengeance drives emotional behaviors. Decision-making is flawed when people are under the influence of vengeance. Their perception of reality is distorted. Peace is seen as weak. Negotiation is seen as capitulation on sacred values. Vengeance is the first, primal need of every victim.

Vindication

Vindication is the need to be right. Victims often feel like they have been wronged, and so there is an intense need for vindication. This need drives people to lawsuits for the sole reason of proving they are right and the other person is wrong.

Validation

Validation is the need to be respected and honored as a human being. Victims often experience despair, grief, and feelings of abandonment. Their need for validation is to overcome the negative emotions and feel good about themselves. Validation restores self-esteem, honor, and dignity.

To Be Heard

The need to be heard is not only about having one's story heard. It is also about being heard at a deep, empathic level. Blocking, which I discussed earlier in this chapter, is when a victim repeats the story over and over again. Blocking indicates that the victim has not been heard at a sufficiently deep level. The repetitive story-telling is an unconscious attempt to process and come to grips with difficult emotional memories. You may guess that affect labeling and core messaging are the surest ways of helping meet a victim's need to be heard.

To Create Meaning

We are reality-creating beings. Our brains make sense of the world by fabricating a story that helps us understand what is going on around us. For a victim, the story line has been severely disrupted. There is no longer a way to make sense of the world because a traumatic event has broken assumptions, expectations, and beliefs about how things are. To gain a sense of control and stability, victims have a need to create meaning out of the mess they find themselves in. Sometimes, this meaning is religious; sometimes it is to take on a conflict like a holy crusade on jihad. The need to create meaning becomes all-consuming as some transcendent goal is chosen and pursued. Many conflicts have been driven by this unmet need.

Safety

Victims often feel threatened physically and emotionally. Their perceptions of a safe, soothing world have been shattered. They seek out ways of coping with the ever-present fear, which includes addictive behaviors of all types: depressive, avoidant, hostile, or aggressive behaviors. All of these behaviors are unconscious tactics to deal with the need to be safe.

Meeting the Victim's Needs

Remarkably, if a victim's need to be heard is satisfied, all of the other needs are satisfied as well. Even more remarkable, the need for vengeance disappears. I have seen this transformation in hundreds of conflicts and have had many others tell stories of how victims climbed onto a path of healing after being affect labeled. Deep listening doesn't always work the first or twentieth time. However, it works so well most of the time that it is my go-to tactic in helping victims deal with conflict.

Let's see how we might use the knowledge of the six needs of victims to work with a difficult ex-spouse over parenting issues.

The first step is to recognize that your ex-spouse feels victimized. It makes no difference that you were a saint or a devil in the marriage. This means that you cannot become defensive when accused and attacked. Of course, you feel defensive and perhaps even angry.

However, if you want to salvage a bad situation, you have to control your feelings and help meet your ex's victim needs. You can only solve problems after your ex has been calmed down.

You might be thinking, "Why the heck should I meet my ex's needs?" Only one reason: to protect your children. You have to find a way to build a cooperative parenting relationship. This requires you to stretch yourself to accommodate a person who is not acting very nice. You do not have to be a marshmallow, and you certainly do not have to cave in to demands. You do have to put yourself in an emotional space where you can be nonjudgmental and nonreactive for the few minutes of conversation you have with your ex.

Here is a classic scenario and how it might play out. In this case, I'm choosing the mother as the victim, but it could just as easily be the father.

Your Ex (X): "I love my children. If the court can't protect them from you, I will. I know it's a matter of time before you abuse them. The children are frightened of you. If they don't want to see you, I'm not going to force them. They are old enough to make up their own minds."

You (Y): "You are angry."

X: "Yes, I am. You are a dirty, lying, stinking SOB."

Y: "You feel betrayed and disrespected."

X: "There is no way the children are going to spend a minute with you. I don't care if I end up in jail."

Y: "You are frightened and scared. You feel completely alone and abandoned."

X: "Nobody is on my side. I have to be strong and stand up for the kids. No one else loves them."

Y: "You feel unloved and unsafe. You are all alone."

X: "Yes!"

In this exchange, the mom is using the kids as a way to express what she cannot directly express herself—her intense feelings of betrayal and abandonment. The direct insult is met by an affect label that reflects what the mom is experiencing without any acceptance of blame, denial, or defensiveness. This is really hard to do in the beginning. Everything in you is screaming to fight back. However, if you can maintain your control and follow the feelings, you will find a much better outcome in a lot shorter time. The reality is that, even with brilliant affect labeling, you may not make much of a difference. It's worth the try, however.

If your ex is going to have a chance at healing, she needs someone to listen to her. Here is the same scenario, only you are a friend, not the ex-husband.

> **Your Friend (F):** "I love my children. If the court can't protect them from their abusive father, I will. Even though he's never abused the children, I know it's a matter of time. The children are frightened of their father. If they don't want to see him, I'm not going to force them. They are old enough to make up their own minds."
>
> **You (Y):** "You are extremely angry at your ex and frustrated that the court is not doing more to protect your kids."
>
> F: "Yes. He is a dirty, lying, stinking SOB."
>
> Y: "You hate your ex and feel enormous grief and sadness."
>
> F: "Yeah. Sometimes it's overwhelming."
>
> Y: "You are overwhelmed by your hatred, anger, frustration, and sadness. You feel completely alone and misunderstood."
>
> F: "Exactly."

This time, as a friend, you can go a little deeper. It only takes a few exchanges to get to the bottom of the problem: she is overwhelmed by her negativity and feels completely alone and misunderstood. These are classic manifestations of unmet victim needs. Your empathic listening to her feelings, while ignoring her words, has helped her take a step toward healing her wounds.

Chapter Summary

This chapter has applied affect labeling to our most intimate and personal relationships—partners, spouses, and ex-spouses—when intense arguments and fights occur. We learned:

- About the root causes of our emotional pain and how that plays out in our dysfunctional behaviors
- That in our intimate relationships, we need to practice patience and empathic listening and know when to take a pause, back off, and try again another time
- That divorce can be rife with intense emotions and anger, especially when coparenting
- About the six needs of victims and how this understanding can be especially useful when dealing with a vengeful person, like an ex-spouse

7

Be an Affect Label Leader

This course is incredibly powerful and has given me many tools for my life and mediation practice. Every mediator and lawyer—any person, in fact—would benefit from this training.

—**Marney Lutz**

De-escalating at Work

Most people spend the majority of their waking hours at work. Although we may choose where we work, we don't necessarily get to choose who we work with or who works around us. Consequently, there is bound to be annoyance, friction, and conflict.

The conflicts may become worse if supervisors and managers lack leadership skills. Leadership and supervision are entirely different skills: leadership makes conflict an asset while management makes conflict something to be avoided. The net result of conflict avoidance is unhappiness and lack of productivity.

In this chapter, we apply the basic skills of affect labeling with a:

- Coworker
- Boss
- Subordinate

How to Affect Label a Coworker

There are times when coworkers drive you crazy. Learning how to listen to their emotions rather than their words may provide relief from their annoying behavior. As always, follow the formula:

1. Ignore the words.
2. Listen to and reflect back the emotions.

By listening in this new way, you will engage in some counterintuitive situations. When you might want a coworker to go away and leave you alone or stop an annoying behavior, you might consider listening to his or her emotions. Your coworkers bring all of their life experiences and emotional baggage to work with them. Annoying behavior is the programming that has been learned at home. While you might wish for more adultlike, reasonable manners, remember that you are with a human being who may not have had a positive emotional life experience. Your job is not to fix this person. You simply are trying to calm things down, so everyone can get back to the business at hand.

The first scenario is the coworker who throws tantrums and argues with everyone. There could be many causes for this person's way of being around others. If you decide to listen to the emotions, you might be able to tap into a root cause and soothe your colleague into peace. Here's one way you might deal with a ranting coworker:

> **Jim (J)**: "This is just BS. Here they go again, making us do this stupid crap. I've had it with them. They are a bunch of idiots. And why the hell do you roll over for them? What kind of a wussy are you anyway?"
>
> **You (Y)**: "Jim, you are pissed off!"
>
> **J**: "Damn right I am. Tired of those bastards upstairs dictating to us how to do our jobs!"
>
> **Y**: "You feel disrespected and not listened to."
>
> **J**: "Yeah! They never listen to us. We're just a bunch of cheap, replaceable gears in their big machine!"
>
> **Y**: "You feel like you don't have a voice and are treated unfairly."
>
> **J**: "Not treated unfairly. Just disrespected, like we aren't worth sh*t."
>
> **Y**: "So you feel like you are treated like sh*t by management. And you feel unappreciated."
>
> **J**: "Exactly. I never know what they want, and directions change all the time. I don't know what the hell to do. Why don't they just leave us alone to do our jobs?"
>
> **Y**: "You are anxious and confused and simply want to be left alone to do your job."
>
> **J**: "Yep. Is that too much to ask?"

Y: "You feel like a prisoner with no freedom to act, and that feels very disrespectful to you."

J: "You got it!"

No matter what Jim says, you ignore the words and reflect his feelings. A couple of times, he asks you a question. You ignore the question and reflect his feelings under it. This is very important. Often, people will unconsciously ask a question. Your reactive response is to answer it. Once you do that, you are in your coworker's game and out of yours.

The trick is to ignore questions and focus on emotions. If the question is important, you can circle back to it after you have de-escalated your coworker. Sometimes, argumentative coworkers will insult or attack you. This could be inflammatory if you listen to the words. If you ignore the words, they have no effect on you. You may actually feel some compassion for this unpleasant coworker.

Another common annoyance is the coworker who talks all of the time. By now, you might recognize the underlying cause: a deep need to be heard and to connect. You have to handle this person with some discernment. If you listen deeply, you might find this coworker glued to you the entire day. He may be so needy that you are like a cup of water in a vast desert. If that's the case, you must set boundaries with him and be firm. Amazingly, he probably then complies because he is feeling heard. Assuming that is not the case, you may be successful at calming the talker down simply by reflecting his emotions.

Here's one example of how that might happen:

Anna-Marie (A-M): "And you know how Susie was in the workroom last week. She just can't seem to get enough of him. Well, I never thought I would see the day. And my daughter was telling me just last night how her three-year-old is such a darling. Don't you just love children when they are at that age? Did you hear about the new push to increase productivity? I wonder where they think we will find the time. I wish they'd hire more people, so we wouldn't have to stress so much. Jessica over there is wondering whether she wants to go for that promotion. She is so talented, but I don't think she's ambitious enough."

You (Y): "You are anxious."

A-M: "Well, no. Not really. Did you hear how Roger's boy was beaten up at school? And that food last week in the commissary! I can't imagine what they were thinking. It was just awful. Quarterly results are due next week, and Bill is really worried about our group's performance. His bonus depends on good results, and he is really crazed about it."

Y: "You are nervous about the performance results."

A-M: "Well, yeah. Aren't you? I mean, it's important to us all."

Y: "You are worried and afraid that we won't be respected."

A-M: "Of course."

There is always the question of what to do with people who talk so much that you cannot get a word in edgewise. Here's where affect labeling really shines. You can interrupt without fear of being rude or inconsiderate as long as you stay with "You" statements and focus on emotions.

The normal conventions around conversations simply do not apply with affect labeling because affect labeling is not conversation. Think about it. In normal conversations, you and your friend or coworker are normally exchanging words. You are waiting for a pause to take your turn. You agree, disagree, change subjects, or take any number of acceptable and polite conversational gambits, depending on the situation. You would be rude to interrupt and impose your point of view before the other person has finished.

In affect labeling, however, you are not in the conversation. The only person in the conversation is the speaker, and you are simply reflecting back the emotions in simple, direct sentences. You may "interrupt" as often as you think is appropriate with an affect label.

Don't take my word for it. Experiment on a talker. Give the talker some space to rant on about something and interrupt occasionally with an affect label. Observe the speaker's reaction.

When I demonstrate this in my classes and workshops, everyone except the speaker thinks I am the rudest, most arrogant, presumptuous listener they have ever seen. Then I ask the speaker what her experience was like. Invariably, she will say something like, "I have never been so deeply listened to before in my life."

The students are stunned and disbelieving. Interrupting is such a basic rude behavior that they cannot imagine how any utterance, when it interrupts the speaker, could be completely affirming and validating. This is another reason why affect labeling is counterintuitive. Because it is not conversation, the rules of conversation do not apply. But it looks like conversation, so it would seem that the rules should apply. Like I said, don't take my word for it. Try it out in a safe, low-risk situation and see for yourself what happens.

Affect labeling this way is the only method I have discovered to work with incessant talkers. As a mediator, I often work under tight time constraints. If I had to wait for talkers to get through, we would never have time to solve the problems at hand. By affect labeling as the talker rambles on, I am able to calm something deep inside. Quickly, the speaker loses the need to run on and on.

Another common coworker is the one with the dark clouds over her head. Always negative, this person never has a good day and makes sure that everyone around her knows it. The negativity is probably habitual. Underneath, however, it's likely that this person is both sad and isolated. A little affect labeling might brighten her day and let in a little sun, so everyone can take a breath.

Here's an example of how you might go about it:

Melinda (M): "I'm having another crummy day. My cat is sick, and my mother is bugging me to visit. Everyone is always so demanding of me."

You (Y): "You are sad and unhappy. You are feeling unfulfilled."

M: "Yeah. And I have this terrible headache that just won't go away."

Y: "You are feeling alone and isolated."

M: "Yeah. Life is pretty bad right now."

Y: "You feel despair."

M: "Yeah, exactly. How did you know? Thanks for listening."

Another obnoxious personality type is the person who uses jargon in place of critical thinking. People use jargon as a substitute for planning, thinking, and designing executable strategies. They often use jargon to avoid the hard work of giving clear directions to their colleagues. Sometimes, affect labeling can penetrate the jargon and help your colleague do some real problem-solving.

Aaron (A): "Well, you know we will have to land and expand with the new client with some blue-sky thinking outside the box. It will take a helicopter view with our ducks in a row. But if we're successful, we will really have an end-user perspective that will help us push the envelope and maybe even boil the ocean."

You (Y): "You are excited and anxious.

A: "We'll have to get someone to do the heavy lifting in engineering, which will take some face time downstairs in the cubicle farm. Hopefully, we will be able to pick the low-hanging fruit on this one."

Y: "You're anxious and not sure that you will be supported. You are a little fearful that this might not work."

A: "Yeah. How'd you know that?"

Y: "Just listened to you, that's all. Want to do some problem-solving?"

A: "Yeah. That'd be nice. Thanks."

Aaron uses jargon incessantly to cover up his insecurity and anxiety over a new project. Rather than just admit that he is challenged, which would require some scary vulnerability, he resorts to trite phrases and euphemisms to sound cool and in control. Your first instinct might be to blow him off, like you have in the past. With affect labeling, you might be able to help him move through his anxiety. Why would you do that? Because you don't want to listen to the jargon anymore. Or you need him to succeed in this new project. Or you need his help on another project and want to connect with him to create some collaboration. There are lots of reasons to affect label the insecure jargon pusher. Of course, you can always choose to not listen either. Now, however, you have some new choices about what you can do with Aaron.

No matter where you work, you are likely to encounter an arrogant colleague who uses sarcasm or a patronizing tone when speaking to you. This person may be infuriating because sarcasm and patronization are disrespectful. Working with this person is challenging because you have to, first, keep your cool and, second, want to do something positive.

Know-it-alls have an innate need to be right. They use sarcasm as a wall to protect their self-esteem. As you might expect, underneath the sarcasm are unconscious emotions driving the attitude. Unchecked, these people are a source of stress and annoyance. Affect labeling may help deflect some of the sarcasm, so you can establish a reasonable working relationship.

You (Y): "Hey, Rebecca, could you explain that procedure to me? I'm not sure I get it yet."

Rebecca (R): "Jeez. It's so simple even a two-year-old could get it.
I don't know what your problem is."

Y: "You are frustrated and put out right now."

R: "Yeah. I mean, anybody with half a brain could figure this out
in two seconds."

Y: "You are annoyed that others can't figure this out."

R: "Yeah, I'm annoyed. Okay, let's do this one more time."

Y: "You are frustrated that not everyone is as smart as you."

R: "Exactly."

Y: "And you feel disrespected that the company doesn't value you."

R: "Yeah. How'd you know that?"

Y: "Ha! You just told me."

R: "Well, thanks for getting it. Maybe you aren't as dumb as you
look."

Y: "You're welcome."

This person is difficult to be with, no question. If you don't have
to work with this person and are not dependent upon her, avoid her
when you can. When you have no choice, try affect labeling to see
if you can shift her attitude toward you. It won't always work, but it
beats putting up with the hurtful insults and sarcasm.

Every difficult coworker is experiencing emotions that are causing dysfunctional behaviors. These behaviors have been learned
as coping strategies for insecurity, anxiety, fear, sadness, and low
self-esteem. Once you recognize the underlying emotional patterns,
you may choose to use some affect labeling to calm them down. You
should find that your colleagues become a little easier to tolerate.

How to Affect Label a Boss

Working under someone else's supervision has an inherent problem:
you lose autonomy. In other words, when you work for someone
else, you can't always do what you want to do. You have to do what

your boss wants and put your own desires aside. If you have a boss who is emotionally unintelligent, a poor leader, or emotionally dysfunctional (as many people are), your life at work may sometimes be miserable.

When you have a boss who is a true leader, you don't mind giving up some autonomy because following this person is a true joy. You feel like you can actually accomplish a lot more with this leader in charge than you ever could on your own. A good leader helps create meaning in your life, and you cherish that.

Bosses who lack emotional intelligence tend to avoid conflict. They haven't developed the ability to confront uncomfortable situations and find it easier to just tune you out. They blame you when things go wrong, even though they were unavailable when leadership was required. They may have learned this behavior in childhood, or it may have worked as a career strategy.

Listening to a boss is a delicate thing. If you are too heavy-handed, your boss feels manipulated. You must exercise skill and discernment when you decide to affect label a superior. Generally, less is more. A quick throwaway label is better than digging into the emotional trenches. On the other hand, if you have a good relationship with your boss, going deeper may be a useful service you provide. Plenty of subordinates have advanced quickly in organizations by making themselves invaluable sounding boards and listeners to their superiors. With these general considerations in mind, let's look at some common scenarios and how affect labeling might be of use.

The first situation is the boss who is rude, disrespectful, and a bully. Here is a person who has no people skills. This boss does not understand leadership and believes that coercion through threats is the only reliable way to motivate subordinates. This boss makes your working life unpleasant. How might you delicately use affect labeling with such a boss? Remember, as with all new skills, if you are too obvious, you will be caught. At the least, you will be embarrassed and ridiculed. At the worst, you will be reprimanded and treated henceforth as untrustworthy. Proceed with caution.

George (G): "What the hell is wrong with you people?"
You (Y): "George, you are really pissed off."
G: "Goddamn right I am. You are all a bunch of incompetent fools!"
Y: "You feel completely let down and unsupported."
G: "I sure as hell do."
Y: "You are frustrated and anxious that things aren't getting done."
G: "Exactly."
Y: "Got it. Do you have a few moments to problem-solve through this?"
G: "We don't need to problem-solve. You all just need to do your damn jobs!"
Y: "So, you are feeling disrespected and isolated because people aren't doing their jobs."
G: "Exactly right."
Y: "Okay. Would you be willing to help solve the problem?"
G: "Hell no. You guys created the problem. I expect you to fix it."
Y: "You are feeling impatient and anxious and need the job done now."
G: "That's it."
Y: "All right. We will work on it."
G: "It's about time!"

This boss is so self-absorbed that there is little chance right now of doing any problem-solving. However, some interesting things happen in this exchange.

You start off by not responding to the insult. You choose to ignore the words and pay attention to George's feelings. That saves you from becoming upset and angry. Your choice also prevents the situation from escalating into a shouting match that you would probably lose.

You offer up problem-solving after George seems to respond favorably to your affect label. This only re-escalates George. This happens sometimes. You think you have someone calmed down and try to move into a problem-solving mode, only to find that the person is fired up again. Your response here is perfect: you go back to affect labeling.

You try again to engage George and find that he is not in the engaging mood. Rather than become reactive yourself, you gracefully retreat. This is a great example of affect labeling to keep you from getting sucked into George's emotions. You can't engage him because he does not want to be engaged. At this moment, you take leadership of the situation and choose a course of action designed to de-escalate. That is what subordinates working for bullies often have to do. Notice that you do not back down. You are not intimidated by George. Instead, you hang with him for as long as it seems productive, then back off. If he wants to live in his own upset, you have to let him be that way. However, you don't have to let his anger affect your life.

If this is a pattern that persists, you need to transfer out from under George or find another job. However, you may find that repeated affect labeling brings George around to a place where some real problem-solving can take place. It's pretty clear that George is the problem, not the team.

Another related scenario is the boss who won't listen. She likes to hear herself talk, thinks too highly of her own intellect, or lacks emotional intelligence. The truth is that she can't listen because she has never been heard. The emotions running through this boss may be disrespect, anger, feelings of injustice, sadness, isolation, and abandonment. If you can ignore her words and focus on her emotional experience, you might help her break the cycle. If nothing else, an incremental improvement in her listening might significantly improve your work environment.

Here's a possible scenario:

You (Y): "Andrea, when you dismiss me or cut me off, I feel like I am not being listened to. This causes me to feel frustrated, disrespected, and isolated from you."

Andrea (A): "Well, of course. You are always trying to control everything and everyone. It's a wonder that anyone gets anything done around here. You are such a busybody, getting into everyone's business—of course people are going to ignore you. I certainly have learned to do that with you."

Y: "Hmmm. You feel disrespected."

A: "Yes, because you do disrespect me. How can anyone be otherwise around you? You only care about yourself and not about the team. It's your way or the highway. No space for anyone else at all."

Y: "You don't feel listened to or heard and don't feel supported or appreciated."

A: "Uh-huh. By the way, I need that report from your team tomorrow, not next week. The client meeting was pushed up this morning, and the VP wants time to understand the issues."

Y: "So, you feel ignored and disrespected."

A: "Yes. Will you have the report done tomorrow?"

Y: "I will have the report for you tomorrow."

A: "Good."

This boss is insulting and can't listen. She suddenly changes the subject as if the topic at hand does not exist. She may be unconsciously deflecting herself from her painful emotions triggered by your callout. Your affect labeling keeps you from a response that might be counterproductive: a retort, an argument, or a passive-aggressive retreat. None of those options will work for you in the long run. In this case, Andrea is so out of touch with herself that your affect labeling has little or no effect. She does respond affirmatively to your reflections but does not take the time to process them. Most likely, she is avoiding her feelings. With a boss like this, continue to affect label if only to protect yourself from the poison. By ignoring the words and focusing on her emotions, your ego is much less likely to get involved and be triggered into reactivity.

Another problematic boss is the one who blames everyone else for the slightest blips and miscues and then holds on to the grudge. Ever been blamed when you did everything exactly as directed? You feel a deep injustice at the wrongful accusation. You are right! And you are forgetting the cardinal rule of work. If you don't hold the power, being right is not relevant. We all think we are right, and when we are angry, we think we are righter than ever. This is true for your boss as well as for you. He likes being right just as much as you do. Maybe he likes being right even more, so as to preserve his self-esteem with the organization.

As with so many other situations, the worst thing you can do for yourself when unjustly blamed is to become defensive and argumentative. If you try to justify yourself, you will be perceived as attacking your boss's credibility. This is where affect labeling can preserve your sanity and keep you from losing your temper.

Let's suppose that you received an email from your boss asking you to reserve the large conference room for a meeting. On the day of the meeting, your boss goes to the wrong conference room, thinking that it was the one you reserved. Upon finding out that that room is in use, your boss calls you on the carpet. You are blamed for an error that did not occur. Here's how you might consider handling the situation:

Robert (R): "Look, Conference Room A is completely tied up. I told you last week to reserve it for me. How the hell come you didn't do it?"

You (Y): "Robert, you are really frustrated and angry that the conference room is unavailable for you."

R: "Absolutely. I am really frustrated."

Y: "You feel disrespected and unsupported."

R: "Yes! Why can't I depend on you?"

Y: "You feel like you can't depend on anyone."

R: "Exactly."

Y: "So that I'm clear, which conference room did you ask me to reserve for you?"

R: "Conference Room A."

Y: "Did you change your mind, because the only email I got from you said you wanted to reserve the large conference room. I did that, and I confirmed that it was held for you all day."

R: "Oh."

Y: "Not a problem. I know you have a lot on your plate."

R: "Yeah. Okay. Thanks."

Robert is completely in error and compounds it by blaming you. Rather than get defensive, you affect label him into calm and then ask a simple question. He could have changed his mind and sent you instructions that you never received. When he says, "Oh," he is realizing that he just made a fool of himself. Rather than gloat, you give him a face-saving way out. He still is not adult enough to apologize for his boorishness, but the situation does not escalate any further than it had to.

I mediate a lot of workplace disputes. Many of them revolve around bosses who are difficult. Employees often make a bad situation worse by thinking that they are entitled to be treated with respect. While common decency and good practices should encourage respectful treatment by superiors, there is no entitlement to respect. As I tell employees over and over, it's not illegal to be an unpleasant, difficult boss. When you don't have the power, you may have to put up with a lot of bad behavior. Affect labeling will help you get through the rough spots without you losing your calm.

How to Affect Label a Subordinate

Suppose that you are a leader in an organization. You no doubt have the exact same problems with subordinates that subordinates have with bosses. Human behavior is really quite predictable when looked at from the perspective of emotional experience. As a leader, your eyes will open when you see this. What are the subordinate behaviors that drive you crazy? Here are a few of them:

- Negativity
- Passive-aggressiveness
- High drama
- Combativeness and disrespect
- Dishonesty, lying, and lack of integrity
- Random brain dumps when you are especially busy
- "Not paid to think" syndrome
- Low emotional intelligence

If this list looks a lot like the list of bad boss behaviors, don't be surprised. All of these difficult behaviors are emotionally based unconscious strategies for dealing with pain, frustration, alienation, disrespect, and abandonment. As a boss, you have more latitude with affect labeling because your employees are expected to listen to you, whatever you say.

Affect labeling gives you a tool to turn difficult employees into loyal, productive workers. You can handle hard conversations and escalated feelings cleanly, competently, and professionally. As you experience the power of affect labeling, you learn that it gives you control over many challenging employee situations. You turn high drama toward effective problem-solving and accountable agreements in minutes.

Let's look at some possible scenarios to give you a sense of how affect labeling may be used as a powerful leadership tool.

Nothing kicks down morale like a negative employee. Habitually unhappy people may not realize that their perpetual rainy days are affecting productivity and creativity. They are so accustomed to seeing the world as empty and gray that they are oblivious. Your challenge is to counteract the effect and change the trajectory. Here's how it might work:

You (Y): "Hey, Rachel, how are you feeling today?"

Rachel (R): "Hi. I'm okay. My mother is really sick, and my cat is dying."

Y: "You are anxious and sad."

R: "Yeah. My daughter is dating a jerk who is taking all of her money and treating her like crap."

Y: "You are sad and a little fearful for your daughter."

R: "Yeah, but there's nothing I can do. She doesn't listen to me. Mostly, she ignores my advice."

Y: "You feel alone and abandoned."

R: "Yeah, I do. No one wants to be around me."

Y: "You feel isolated and unappreciated."

R [sighing]: "Exactly. Thanks for listening."

This short bit of affect labeling demonstrates a common behavior: the inability to respond to the question "How do you feel?" Most people do not have sufficient self-awareness to describe their emotional experience at any given time. If their experience is strong enough, they are forced to pay attention and then can say something about how they feel. For Rachel, being depressed is normal, so she cannot process it sufficiently to answer your question. Instead, she substitutes an answer to an unasked question when she responds, "Yeah. My daughter is dating a jerk who is taking all of her money and treating her like crap." It's like she did not even hear you, and she probably did not. The secret is to not give up or become frustrated.

In this example, you stick with Rachel. Whatever emotion comes up, you label, whether Rachel is aware of it or not. Eventually, you reach the core issue when you say, "You feel isolated and unappreciated." Rachel relaxes with a sigh. Finally, some part of her recognizes that she has been deeply heard.

Why take the time to do this work? First, look at the real time investment. This conversation might take thirty to forty-five seconds, maximum. If you took another approach, such as to counsel Rachel or advise her not to be so negative, you would be in for a much longer conversation. By starting with affect labeling, you are saving yourself time.

Second, think about your role as a leader. As much as you might resist the idea, the people you lead need you to be a psychological anchor for them. This doesn't mean that you are a therapist or provide a shoulder to cry on every day. It means that you are paying attention to your employees' emotional experiences. How your employees are feeling during the day directly affects their productivity and your bottom line profitability. You might minimize the importance of feelings at work, and you would be making a classic leadership mistake. All decision-making, all reasoning, all problem-solving starts with emotion.

Without emotion, we cannot choose, cannot decide, and cannot be rational. Likewise, if we experience intense emotion, we may freeze, see limited options, and make nonrational decisions. The optimally performing team is one whose general emotional experience is in the zone of maximum effectiveness. Your principal job as a leader is to monitor where people are in relation to that zone and help them stay in it. Affect labeling is your go-to tool for the task.

Bosses think they have power, and maybe they do. But so do employees. Without the employees' willing cooperation, nothing gets done. I asked a group of midlevel leaders at a large auto dealership company who they thought had the most power in the room. As we went around, I saw something that they did not.

"You guys still don't see it. Who in this room has the power over your commission checks and revenue streams?" They were baffled. No one seemed to have that power.

"What about Patty back there? She is the finance contract manager for the entire firm. Every contract goes across her desk. Patty, what happens if you decide to delay a contract for a day or so?"

Patty said, "It doesn't get processed with the lender, and we don't get paid for the sale."

"And if that happens?" I asked.

"No payment, no commissions, no salaries," she said.

"What if you became annoyed with one of the VPs or sales managers in the room and held back on their contracts for a few days?" I asked.

She smiled and said, "They don't get paid."

"So, who has the most power in the room?" I asked again. My point was made. Patty appeared to be the least powerful person in the room, a step up from a clerical worker. However, her daily decisions deeply affected every person in the room.

Power in the workplace is widely distributed. As a leader, you have to recognize that and deal with the occasional employee who decides to wield power against you. The classic example of this abuse is the passive-aggressive employee.

Passive-aggressive employees tend to be antagonistic in non-aggressive ways. The passive-aggressive employee intends to control, injure, or create negative impressions of superiors while avoiding responsibility. When confronted, the passive-aggressive person will seem surprised to hear that there is an issue. He or she will claim innocence and deflect blame elsewhere with plausible deniability.

This behavior comes in several flavors. The backstabber employee is one who is compliant and uncomplaining in your presence and then is harshly negative and contemptuous of you in your absence. The just-good-enough employee is the person who purposefully falls just short of compliance—but only to a point that complaining about it seems trivial. The saboteur employee is one who claims to have forgotten something, faults others, subtly expresses disdain, and makes mistakes to cast you in an unfavorable light. The crisis-resolver employee is the person looking for the right time to save the day. This person waits until you are away to create a crisis. He or she goes over your head to your manager, seeking approval from higher authority for necessary actions. The intention is to create an appearance that you are unreliable, and he or she is accountable.

Passive-aggressive people are not simply bad eggs with nothing better to do than make other people look bad. Often, they suffer from an emotional catalyst. Without taking time to identify what is going on emotionally, you are doomed to misery. Affect labeling is one tool that might help you turn around a bad situation.

Here's a potential way of confronting and managing a passive-aggressive employee:

You (Y): "Thanks for meeting with me, Alfonso."
Alfonso (A): "Sure. No problem."
Y: "Look, I have a potential problem that I want to explore with you."
A: "Okay.
Y: "I heard a lot of reports, and by a lot, I mean more than a dozen, that you are criticizing me and my decisions behind my back. I'm confused because in meetings, you always seem to support my decisions. I have never heard you object or take issue with anything. I am just wondering what is going on."
A: "Yeah, well, it's all a pack of lies. Anybody who is saying bad things about me is full of crap!"
Y: "You are angry."

A: "Yeah, I'm angry. No one should be dissing me."

Y: "You feel disrespected."

A: "Yeah."

Y: "And you feel betrayed, like someone is ratting you out."

A: "Damn straight I am."

Y: "So, tell me how you feel about working for me."

A: "It's okay, I guess."

Y: "You are frustrated."

A: "A little. Sometimes."

Y: "You feel disrespected and unappreciated."

A: "Yeah."

Y: "You don't feel listened to and don't feel like your opinions count."

A: "Yeah, exactly. You always know it all and never listen."

Y: "You feel that the situation is unfair and that you should have more of a voice."

A: "Yeah."

Y: "You feel like others would look up to you."

A: "Yeah."

Y: "You've been here a long time and feel like that should count for something."

A: "Exactly."

Y: "You are frustrated that you've been passed over for promotions."

A: "Yup."

Y: "You just don't feel like your worth is valued here."

A [sighing]: "Yeah, that's it exactly."

You can get to the truth of the matter without being confrontational. When you take a small leap and say, "And you feel betrayed, like someone is ratting you out," Alfonso admits that he is angry that someone called out his behavior. This is as close to an admission that you will get from Alfonso, and it's all you really need. Once he confirms through his acknowledgment of the emotions you are labeling that he was criticizing you behind your back, you can move on. And that's what happens.

You say, "So, tell me how you feel about working for me." This is a new technique that builds on what you have learned. When you have created some emotional safety by not chewing Alfonso out, you have the opportunity to probe for the deeper problem. One way to do this is to ask how someone is feeling about something. Regardless of the verbal response, you can read the emotions and label them back. This leads you on a path of discovery to the root cause. In this case, Alfonso's passive-aggressive behavior is based on his anger at not being promoted, his feeling that his seniority is not being respected, and his self-perceived worth not being appreciated. His coping strategy for blunting the emotional pain this caused him is to sabotage you. When you finally get there, he involuntarily engages his relaxation response. Alfonso feels some relief that you finally get his feelings about being passed over and disrespected. This is good. And it is the point at which you can start doing some relationship repair work through problem-solving.

Compare this way of dealing with Alfonso with the typical strategy. Most bosses would confront, accuse, and threaten him. He would deny any wrongdoing. Nothing would be accomplished except you would both be more mistrustful, angry, and frustrated. Alfonso would probably double down on his passive-aggressive behavior. Your working relationship would become more toxic, not less.

The Nature of Leadership

Listening, affect labeling, and problem-solving in the arena of our work and professional world offers us an opportunity to be leaders, whatever our position and role. However, it's important to be clear what it means to be a leader in this context. We tend to throw around the word *leadership* carelessly, confusing it with authority, management, and power. Leadership really has little to do with authority, management, and power, although they are tools that an effective leader might use.

Leadership, in my view, is the set of skills that one uses to help a group achieve a goal. I believe there are four dimensions to leadership:

1. We may lead up and thus become leaders to organizational superiors.
2. We may lead down and thus become leaders to organizational inferiors.
3. We may lead left and right and thus become leaders to our organizational peers.
4. We may lead inside and thus lead ourselves.

If we are not leading in all four dimensions, we may find ourselves ineffective at helping a group achieve its goal.

Leaders provide three important psychological services to a group:

1. Direction
2. Protection
3. Role Orientation

A leader provides direction by identifying the challenge to the group and engaging the group in a process to understand the problem and the potential range of solutions. A leader provides protection by disclosing external threats to the group and helping the group respond to the threat. A leader provides role orientation by allowing each member of the group to use the leader as an anchor to create identity.

Leaders also work with group conflict. Unlike an authority, who tends to restore order with power and thus avoid conflict, a leader will allow the conflict to emerge and use it to understand better the needs of the group. In all of these roles, leaders confront strong emotions. Knowing how to de-escalate those emotions is a foundational leadership skill.

Chapter Summary

In this chapter, we have learned:

- How to affect label at work or any professional or organized setting, including staff and authority figures: coworkers, bosses, and subordinates
- How to read emotions and affect label at work, an invaluable asset and skill that can directly influence productivity and profitability
- Affect labeling is based on hard neuroscience that effectively and efficiently gets to the root of many interpersonal workplace conflicts.
- Leadership is built upon the abilities to: direct, protect, role orient, and work with group conflict; having the skills to confront strong emotions and swiftly de-escalate a person or situation is a powerful tool for any leader.

8

The Power of Self-Awareness

I'm actually pleasantly surprised at just how learning to listen and reflect back emotions changes the dynamics of relationships. For myself, these newfound skills have enhanced my relationship with my parents. In fact, recently I have been having to endure some difficult family issues, and it's interesting because on separate occasions, both of my parents said to me, "When did you become so smart, and how do you know all of these things?" These statements made me feel tremendously good. My relationships as a whole have improved, and I'm so thrilled. I've even noticed that my mood has stabilized. I'm not as moody. I'm a more pleasant, less stressed/irritated person. I have more patience and compassion toward people as well, and I'm learning to articulate myself more efficiently as well.

—**Anna Humiston**, Valley State Prison for Women[14]

When I began to teach inmates serving life sentences these skills, I expected them to defuse potentially violent arguments quickly and effectively. Within weeks of learning the skills, that is exactly what happened. Several months into the training, something else even more magical happened. Inmates began reporting that they were no longer easily provoked. They were not losing their tempers. They were not getting into fights. Instead, they were naturally affect labeling themselves.

This unexpected benefit led my colleague Laurel Kaufer and me to think about adding a new module on self-awareness to our peacemaker training curriculum. We had a section on managing strong emotions already, so it was simply a matter of developing all of the ideas into a teachable unit. The results were spectacularly transformative. As inmates gained insights into their triggers and actively practiced self-affect labeling, they found inner peace and calm. For many, it was another life-changing moment in our Prison of Peace Project.

Developing Emotional Intelligence

There are thousands of articles and hundreds of books on how to develop emotional self-awareness. Emotional self-awareness is the foundation for emotional intelligence. Yet it seems to be a skill in short supply. I believe the reason is based on the fact that, as children, we are not systematically taught how to be self-aware. Instead, as I revealed in chapter 2, we are victims of emotional invalidation. We are taught that our emotions are bad, irrational, and scary. We are taught that we cannot be rational if we are emotional first.

We are not taught that emotions are what make us human, not our limited capacity to reason. As a result, learning to become self-aware of our emotional experiences is dependent upon our personal motivations. Usually, we focus on developing self-awareness because the pain of unconscious emotions and the destructive behaviors they may cause propels us to look inward, but what happens when we don't have that self-motivation?

Emotional self-awareness is a complex cognitive function. Recall that in chapter 1, psychologist Silvan Tomkins stated that humans are born with nine affects. Affects are the biological responses created in the brain to events happening in our immediate environment. Here are his nine affects again:

Interest-Excitement
Enjoyment-Joy
Surprise-Startle
Fear-Terror
Distress-Anguish
Anger-Rage
Disgust
Dissmell
Shame-Humiliation

These are the raw biological responses that infants display. They are not learned responses. Instead, they appear to be innate responses to the environment. Over many months, these affects are associated with basic emotions. Emotions are cognitive structures that associate affect and feeling in a simple label. By creating even the simplest label, we learn to express what we are experiencing. At a rudimentary level, we think about what is causing us to feel emotion and take action to experience either more or less of the emotion, depending on the situation. The creation of these cognitive labels is called emotional categorization and, unlike affect, is learned from experience.

As we mature, and if we are lucky, we slowly take broad categories of emotion and subdivide them into smaller, more refined grades. This process is called emotional granularization.[15] We create emotional granularization through exposure, directly and vicariously, to many different emotional experiences. One of the reasons reading great literature is a precondition to an educated mind is because of the emotional experiences the author gives the reader. It starts with something as simple as *Winnie the Pooh* and culminates in the extraordinary emotional complexity of *Moby Dick*.

The sticking point is that somewhere along the way, we fail to associate our emotional experiences with the vast vocabulary of emotions we have learned through education. Most of us are able to name twenty or thirty emotions, if we take the time to think about it. However, when asked how we feel, we only use five or six emotions to describe our state. Self-awareness is the ability to describe with particularity what emotions we are experiencing in any given moment, especially when we are experiencing strong emotions.

The task of developing self-awareness is to connect our real-time emotional experiences with the words that describe the experience. The emotionally self-aware person is able to examine her emotional experiences in the moment and describe them to herself or others.

The benefits of this skill are numerous and important.

First, the better we granularize our emotions, the clearer we are about what we are experiencing. We are able to concretize emotional experience in our conscious awareness. This reduces anxiety, promotes certainty, and aids in higher cognitive processing. Second, emotional granularity allows us to assess cause and effect more accurately. Being able to distinguish among anxiety, annoyance, and frustration, for example, tells us a lot about what to look for in our immediate environment. Again, this ability reduces anxiety and creates a greater sense of control. Third, we are able to make a more refined choice about how to respond to our emotional experience. Finally, we are able to express clearly how we are feeling and why to others. This is deeply empowering.

Building Your Emotional Granularity

The task of developing self-awareness can be fun, if you go about it the right way. We are fortunate to have access to all kinds of emotional experiences. We simply need to use these as teaching moments. You might recall from chapter 1 that I listened to a radio ad coming through the speakers in a waiting room. On a whim, I decided to label and count the emotions being expressed. I was surprised at how many emotions were expressed in thirty seconds. As I listened, I discovered that ads are intentionally emotional. They are designed and created to motivate us to take action. What a great free learning tool!

Here's an exercise expanding on that:

1. Tune in to a radio station.
2. Listen to what is playing.

If a song is playing, listen to what emotions are being expressed by the artist, the music, and the lyrics. Here's a guide to follow:

- Pop: Sadness, loneliness, lost love (abandonment)
- Country: Sadness, loneliness, lost love (abandonment)
- Hip-hop: Anger, frustration, despair
- Rock: Anger, rage, sadness, loneliness

Label what you are hearing and experiencing by stating the emotion out loud. If an ad is playing, list all of the emotions you hear expressed by the actors.

Practice this exercise a couple of times and notice how your emotional acuity improves. As you listen to people around you, notice that their emotions are coming through loud and clear. More important, after a couple weeks of practicing, you will find that your self-awareness has become more refined.

Here's a second exercise:

1. Watch a television show or movie.
2. For a couple of minutes, label the emotions of the actors in one or two scenes. Don't do this for long because it is tiring, and you will not enjoy the show.
3. As a variation, just listen to the audio portion of the show and label the emotions.
4. Now turn off the sound and watch the actors. Label their emotions based on their nonverbal behaviors.
5. Write down what you observed as a means of associating your emotional vocabulary with your observation. You can find many lists of emotions on the internet.

In not very much time at all, you are creating new associations between your intellectual knowledge of emotions and your experience of emotions. You are developing emotional granularization.

What Triggers You?

The next step is to understand your triggers. Triggers are environmental cues that cause a cascade of past programming to activate automatically and usually unconsciously. Our everyday behaviors are largely unconscious because we have learned thousands and thousands of cognitive schemas for dealing with life. Each schema is like a computer program, although probably quite a bit more complex. These schemas, or scripts, allow us to manage routine and mundane tasks without thinking about them too much.

The downside is that our emotional responses to life are also coded in cognitive schemas. This means that when Uncle Harry starts pontificating about his political views, you are automatically triggered into an emotional experience. You have a set of schemas that are set into play outside of your consciousness. If you are not aware of the emotions released by your schemas, you suffer from the absence of emotional self-awareness.

Although we have tens of thousands of schemas, the ones that really get us into trouble are relatively limited. Developing self-awareness requires us to examine our life experience and identify our triggers. We start with anger and go through some other basic emotions one at a time. The first step is to think about and identify the three situations that make you angry. Write them down on a sheet of paper.

For example, you might write:

1. I get angry when my husband doesn't listen to me.
2. I get angry when my kids don't do what I say.
3. I get angry when my boss dumps a huge project on me at 4:45 in the afternoon.

Then identify when you were last triggered by asking yourself the following questions:

- Where was I?
- What time of day was it?
- Who was around me?
- What did I hear, smell, and see?
- What were my emotions?
- What did I feel physically?
- What was my behavioral reaction (what did I do)?

As you look at what is revealed, are you seeing a recurrent trigger around anger? If so, you can begin to reprogram yourself by asking the following: When I am in this place, at this time, with these people, am I likely to get triggered? If I am triggered, how can I choose to respond to my emotions and feelings?

Complete the statements below:

- When I felt:
- I was probably experiencing:
- My automatic response was:
- My other choices in the moment were:
- The result of my automatic response was:
- A different choice I can consciously make in the future is:

If you take fifteen minutes to work this out, you gain valuable insights into your automatic, unconscious programming. Repeat the exercise for feelings of: frustration, sadness, loneliness, being unloved, and being unworthy. Then reflect and write down what you learned from this exercise.

De-escalating Yourself

Spend a couple hours over a few days doing all of the exercises I have listed and start to see your automatic emotional responses with clarity. As you become aware of an emotional experience arising from a trigger condition, affect label yourself just like you would someone else:

"I am angry."
"I am frustrated."
"I feel disrespected."
"I don't feel heard or listened to."
"I am sad."
"I am afraid."
"I am lonely."
"I feel unloved."
"I feel unworthy."

Affect labeling concretizes your emotional experience into consciousness where you can make choices about how you respond to it. You might make good or bad choices. The key is that you are not acting unconsciously. Knowing this calms you down and slows down automatic reactivity. If you want to work out what choices would be best for you when you are emotionally escalated, do this exercise.

Complete the following sentence for each negative emotion you experience on a regular basis:

When I experience _____, I need
     more _____.
When I experience _____, I need
     more _____.

For example:

- When I am experiencing a lack of inspiration, I need more inspiration.
- When I am experiencing resentment, I need more gratitude [toward that which you resent].
- When I am experiencing victimization, I need to take more responsibility.
- When I am experiencing powerlessness and being out of control, I need to feel more powerful and in control.
- When I am experiencing impatience, I need to feel more patient.

The power of self-affect labeling became clear to me in a conversation I had with an inmate:

"Hey, Doug, you won't believe what happened to me," he said.

"Yeah, Daniel. Do tell."

"Well, I was in med line the other day, and this dude cut right in front of me."

"Pissed you off," I said, using affect labeling.

"Sure did. But here's the cool thing. Normally, I would have gotten crazy mad and gone after him. This time, I paused. I said to myself, 'I'm angry. I feel disrespected. I feel frustrated.' As soon as I affect labeled myself, the emotions went away. I could think about the situation. I decided the guy was a jerk, but not worth getting into a fight about it."

"That's pretty awesome. You felt really proud of yourself that you could figure out what you were feeling and made some conscious choices about how to respond."

"I did," Daniel told me.

"Good job, man. I'm proud of you."

That's when I learned that self-affect labeling really works.

The Transcendent State of Egolessness

In *The Power of Now*, Eckhart Tolle described a belief system created by being present in the moment, with no attention placed on the past or the future. Tolle famously contended that by exercising the power of now, we can free ourselves from our pain-body to live centered lives. He described the pain-body as accumulated pain forming a negative energy that occupies body and mind.[16] I read *The Power of Now* and was disappointed that Tolle did not provide any new tools for achieving the egoless state he advocated. Tolle got there through an enlightenment experience rather than through years of systematic work. However, his ideas around egolessness resonated with me.

I am not sure when it happened; I think it was when I was teaching a workshop. As I demonstrated affect labeling, something strange and wonderful happened to me. I became egoless for the fifteen or twenty seconds I was focusing on a storyteller's emotional experience. My sense of "I" disappeared, and I was aware of my true essence and nothing else. Even though I was affect labeling a participant, I seemed to be transcendent. Of course, I was teaching, so I could not unpack what happened until later.

When I had time to reflect, I realized that by affect labeling I must have entered into what Tolle described as the power of now—the state of pure egolessness. Wow, affect labeling might be a spiritual practice! That was a bonus I had not expected. As with all things connected to my work, I wanted to know if there was any neuroscience behind the experience of egolessness during affect labeling, and after some research and time, a possible explanation was revealed.

Sigmund Freud coined the term *ego* in the early twentieth century and thought it to be the source of consciousness, or the awareness of self. Ego became synonymous with the small "me," and eventually took on negative attributes, such as being selfish, self-centered, and narcissistic. Big egos were ascribed to people who thought highly of themselves and not so highly of those around them.

In the twenty-first century, advanced imaging techniques allowed neuroscientists a far more nuanced idea of what ego was really about. In modern terms, ego is about self-reference—the ability to think about ourselves in relationship to our environment and social relationships. Our ability to self-reference, based in what some researchers call the "self-referencing center," has two components: the reactive self-referencing center and the deliberate self-referencing center.

The reactive self-referencing center, associated with the ventral medial (bottom middle) prefrontal cortex of the brain, is active when we engage in subjective valuation. "Show me the money," or, "What's in it for me," are thoughts and associated emotions that are created in the reactive self-referencing center. This part of the brain receives input from the emotional centers responsible for the reactions of fear and disgust as well as emotional decision-making. Much of the activity is automatic and unconscious. When this part of our brain is active, we experience the ego that Freud hypothesized.

The deliberative self-referencing center, associated with the dorsal (top) prefrontal cortex, is active when we engage in *mentalizing*. Mentalizing occurs when we think about what other people are thinking or feeling. In other words, when we affect label another or experience compassion, we are engaging in a mentalizing process in the deliberative self-referencing center. When the deliberative self-referencing center is active, we do not experience ego; we experience wisdom and egolessness.

Without training and practice, we spend much time with our reactive self-referencing system. Because much of this work is automatic and habitual, it is easy to be here. Mentalizing in the deliberative self-referencing system, by contrast, is much harder work and is not automatic. We have to make a conscious choice to engage in this activity. This helps to explain why affect labeling and core messaging are not part of our everyday experiences. Both skills require effortful thinking and, in the absence of consistent practice, are not habitual.

The great news is that through simple, consistent practice, we can access an egoless state. By affect labeling and core messaging others, we are exercising our deliberative self-referencing center. That exercise builds neural pathways that strengthen over time. In effect, we engage in a deep spiritual practice every time we listen to and label the emotions of another. We are able to experience the power of now by serving others through affect labeling, empathic listening, and core messaging.

I began to test this in workshops. After participants had some experience with affect labeling and core messaging each other, I asked them to pay attention to their own experiences. When we debriefed, some people reported nothing dramatic, but many others were excited over the transcendent experience they had. Although completely anecdotal, the stories matched my own experience. It seemed that there was a similar, replicable experience of egolessness.

Much more research needs to tease out whether there is anything to this experience beyond the subjective feeling of transcendence. However, the frequency of reported experience suggests that there is something going on when we affect label and core message others.

Chapter Summary

In this chapter, we learned:

- How to use affect labeling to de-escalate our own strong emotions
- How to identify common emotional triggers
- How to reprogram ourselves
- How affect labeling and core messaging others allows us to experience the transcendent state of egolessness in a practical and profound spiritual experience

9

A Master Skill for Teachers

I attended the extended training sessions last year. In comparison with all of the trainings my school district provided to all teachers over my past twenty-five years in the district, I found the extended training sessions to be the most valuable and relevant for all stakeholders—hands down.

The training is so relevant and meaningful for all employees (and for all relationships in general) that I would like to recommend that it become a prominent part of our staff development meetings. In addition, it would perhaps be even more awesome to schedule it for all students as a campus-wide rally, and in smaller groups such as what the After School Program offers. Many of our students' parents REALLY need it.

It is so good, I have signed up for the extended sessions again. Making new ways to more effectively relate with people requires practice and support—even more reason for making the training a regular part of our weekly staff development schedule so that all will be able to participate in it as a unified team.

—**Paul Germain**, California high school teacher

De-escalating in the Classroom

Core competencies of any teacher involve classroom management and discipline. In classrooms of thirty students or more, maintaining order is a major challenge. Of those thirty students, some will be ready to learn, others not. Some will be hungry and distracted. Some will be traumatized. Some will be fast learners, others not so fast.

Overcoming students' boredom, keeping kids off smartphones, and engaging them to learn require skill, persistence, and patience. At many schools, teachers don't have time to deal with emotional kids. If an emotional child disrupts the classroom, the accepted recourse is to send the child to administration. What this all adds up to is that implementing effective classroom management can be extremely difficult.

Traditional classroom management has consisted of "trying" to make students behave. In earlier generations, children generally had more respect for authority. For the few students who actively misbehaved, a coercive approach was thought be the best. "Spare the rod and spoil the child," as the saying went. While punishment solved the immediate problem of control, it never solved the underlying problems: What caused the student to misbehave? Why isn't the student engaged and excited about learning? What is going on emotionally in the student?

Modern students have far more information and more independence. They resist authoritarian efforts to curtail misbehavior. In some cases, students up the ante to challenge authority, knowing that a teacher's ability to punish is limited. A trip the principal's office is not a threat; it's a way to get out of an excruciatingly boring environment. Punishment is simply counterproductive. Teachers know this and are frustrated. Students know this and challenge institutional powerlessness.

There are some useful classroom management frameworks for teachers that, coupled with affect labeling, are powerful tools.

These frameworks do not rely on authority or coercion, and they also require development of a set of skills not taught in universities. One of these frameworks, the foundation of the Safe & Civil Schools Project, goes by the acronym STOIC.

It has five components:

1. Structure the classroom for success.
2. Teach students how to behave.
3. Observe student behaviors.
4. Interact positively with students.
5. Correct misbehavior fluidly so that it does not interrupt the flow of instruction.[17]

Affect labeling is the fundamental skill that can effectively be used for the last two components of STOIC: interacting positively with students and correcting misbehaviors fluidly. When you apply affect labeling as a core part of your classroom management skills, you witness dramatic and transformative behavioral changes in your students. As the students watch you affect label emotionally charged situations, they learn how to do for themselves. They assimilate the power of labeling the emotions of others naturally and effortlessly. Before long, they are affect labeling you. When that happens, take credit for teaching them emotional intelligence.

Five social and emotional areas based on emotional intelligence and decision-making behaviors that students need aptitude in to have classroom success are:

1. Self-Awareness
2. Self-Management
3. Social Awareness
4. Relationship Skills
5. Responsible Decision-Making

Ask yourself this question: does every student know how to be a caring, respectful, and responsible member of your school community? Society used to delegate teaching social and emotional skills to the family. Today, families are failing in that task, and the burden is falling on teachers. Your job as a teacher is to make sure your students have opportunities to develop emotional intelligence.

The O in STOIC is for *observe*. But what to observe? For our purposes, anticipate and confirm the emotional experiences of your students. Middle school students, for example, are going through what we all know is a challenging time of life: puberty. As their bodies and brains change with the addition of new hormones and physical growth, their emotional experiences change as well.

On a separate sheet of paper, create a grid with the following headers. List some of the emotional experiences a student might have in each:

- Emotions about Self
- Emotions about Parents and Adults
- Emotions and Cognition
- Emotions about Peers and Friends

Compare notes with other teachers. You will find that students have a limited repertoire of emotions and behaviors. You will see the same emotions and behaviors over and over again. No matter how unique students believe themselves to be, they are highly predictable.

Here's another simple exercise to help you understand the emotional experiences of a student. Complete each of the statements:

- A student did this:
- He or she was probably feeling:
- His or her unmet emotional need was probably:
- My first response to his or her unmet emotional need was to:

- The result of my choice was:
- A different choice I could have made would have been:

When you have prepared yourself by considering the potential range of emotional experiences in your student, you are ready to affect label.

Listening to Students and Parents

The *I* in STOIC is regarding positive interaction with a student, especially one who is misbehaving. Affect labeling is the skill you rely upon frequently. Let's look at some common scenarios and see how affect labeling creates a positive interaction with students.

You have a student who constantly interrupts in class. You have asked her to have a brief conversation with you after class.

> **You (Y):** "Sally, I am wondering what you are feeling when you blurt out and interrupt in class."
> **Sally (S):** "I dunno. It just happens. I can't help myself."
> **Y:** "Okay, how does blurting out make you feel?"
> **S:** "I get excited."
> **Y:** "You are excited."
> **S:** "Yeah. I like to be the first with an answer."
> **Y:** "How does being first with an answer make you feel?"
> **S:** "I feel good."
> **Y:** "So, you feel good. How do you think I feel when you blurt out before I call on you?"
> **S:** "I dunno."
> **Y:** "Well, take a guess. How would you feel if you were me?"
> **S:** "I guess upset and annoyed."
> **Y:** "Right. I am upset and annoyed when you blurt out and interrupt."

S: "Oh."

Y: "You feel good when you interrupt, and I feel annoyed. That doesn't work so well."

S: "I guess not."

Y: "Well, I want you to be excited and feel good in class. And I don't want to feel annoyed. Besides blurting out and interrupting, what else could you do that makes you feel good?"

S: "I dunno. You're the only person who listens to me."

Y: "You don't feel listened to by anyone else. No one at home?"

S: "Nope."

Y: "You are sad because no one pays any attention to you. You feel ignored and alone."

S: "Yeah."

Y: "And you like me paying attention to you, even though you know interrupting annoys me."

S: "Yeah."

Y: "Tell you what. Would you be willing to have a private conversation with just me listening to you after school?"

S: "That would be great!"

Y: "In exchange, would you be willing to control your blurting out and interrupting during class? I won't ignore you, and I will call on you. Just not every time you are the first one with your hand up."

S: "Yeah."

Y: "Good. When would you like to start our conversations?"

S: "Today?"

Y: "Sure. Meet me here after school. Okay?"

S: "Okay. And thank you."

Y: "You're welcome."

Sally must live in an emotionally cold family if she doesn't feel listened to at home. Her blurting out is nothing more than an unconscious strategy for getting her emotional needs met. Others might say that she lacks impulse control, is rude, or is aggressive. Those judgments won't help solve the problem.

In this conversation, you take time to find out what Sally is feeling when she acts out. When you unpack her behavior, she is ready to consider how it affects you. Although she does not affect label you, you assert your annoyance. Rather than telling her to stop her behavior, you state the problem. Sally wants to feel good, and that is causing you to be annoyed. She agrees that the situation is not good. Since the problem seems to be that Sally does not feel listened to by anyone, the solution is straightforward: a short daily conversation when you listen to Sally and deeply satisfy her needs while solving your problem. You probably find that after a few conversations, Sally's needs are met. Her demand on your listening diminishes as she feels validated.

As with so many other aspects of life, investing a little time at the beginning usually pays big dividends in the future. The problem is that the payoff is intangible and uncertain while the upfront cost— your time—is precious and limited. Most people are risk averse. They are not willing to give up their time when there is not an obvious payback. As you practice affect labeling with students, however, you will find that your time investment is insignificant compared with the behavioral changes you see.

Another common classroom situation involves students who are not paying attention. Inattention can be caused by a lot factors. Sometimes listening to what is going on can lead to some deeper insights. Here's another private, after-class conversation. You are listening to learn as well as to validate your student's emotions.

You (Y): "Timothy, we both know you are not paying attention in class. How does being in class make you feel?"
Timothy (T): "I'm pretty bored."

Y: "You are feeling bored and unhappy that you have to be in class."

T: "Yeah. I don't get why we have learn this stuff. It doesn't mean anything to me, so I just tune out."

Y: "How do you feel when you tune out?"

T: "Chill. Relaxed."

Y: "You feel happy and relaxed when you tune out."

T: "Yeah. Exactly."

Y: "What do you need to feel to keep you from tuning out?"

T: "I dunno."

Y: "Well. What would have to happen for you to make this the most exciting part of your day?"

T: "Huh?"

Y: "What would have to happen to make this class the most exciting part of your day?"

T: "I dunno. No one's ever asked me that before."

Y: "Good. Use your imagination and be funny if you want. List off something that would make this class exciting for you."

T: "Well. It would be cool if my friends and I could compete with our video games."

Y: "Interesting. What else?"

T: "Cool music we could jam to."

Y: "Okay. What else?"

T: "I dunno. That would be pretty cool."

Y: "You are pretty excited imagining what class would be like if you could play video games and listen to cool music."

T: "Yeah, that would be very cool."

Y: "Tell you what. I am willing to consider your ideas if you do something for me. Write up a proposal that shows me how to link the material you are learning to your ideas on how to make the class time more exciting."

T: "What do you mean?"

Y: "You are in school to learn. That doesn't mean that it has to be boring all the time. However, I have to have good reasons for deviating from my lesson plan. If you can give me good reasons that I can run past the principal for approval, then maybe we can do something different. Are you willing to write the proposal?"

T: "Yeah. Sure."

Y: "Great. We'll talk more when you get it done. You might want to pay attention in class so that you can figure out how to work in your ideas. If you aren't paying attention, you won't be able to come up with ideas that could really work."

T: "Okay. I see that. Thanks."

Y: "You are welcome."

The likelihood of Timothy coming up with a proposal that works is slim, next to zero, and you know it. That is not the point of the conversation. The purpose is to listen to Timothy at a deep level and engage him. When you listen attentively and do not judge his ideas, he is validated. You open up collaboration by accepting that his ideas might have merit. And you engage him back into the class by asking for a written proposal that has to be approved by someone other than yourself. If Timothy is to write a proposal, he knows it has to be good enough to pass muster with the principal.

Maybe Timothy will pay attention in class, and maybe he won't. However, you have engaged him in a new way. By listening to him, you have respected him. He will respect you and will unconsciously try harder to keep your respect.

Most students are respectful of their teachers. Some are not. How might you positively confront disrespect without giving up your power or authority? Here's a typical scenario:

Student (S): "Screw you!"

You (Y): "You are angry and pissed off."

S: "Damn right I am."

Y: "You feel disrespected."

S: "Yes."

Y: "No one listens to you, and you feel unsupported."

S: "Hmph."

Y: "You are sad because nobody gets you."

S: "Yeah. How did you know that?"

Y: "You feel unloved and unwanted."

S: "Yeah. Exactly. I ain't worth sh*t."

Y: "You feel unworthy of love and feel like you are not worth anything."

S: "Yeah."

Y: "Okay, then."

In tai chi, we use the opponent's energy against him. In affect labeling, the idea is similar. We are using the student's emotions to listen rather than react with our own emotions. In this scenario, you simply reflect your student's emotions that lie underneath the disrespect. As you do so, some important layers surface. What you learn is the student's disrespect is a manifestation of his own self-loathing and lact of self-worth. Instead of reacting to the dis-respect with the traditional authoritarian punishment, you are patient. At the end, your compassion provides a deep teaching moment for your student.

You may be wondering about consequences. There are con-sequences to student misbehavior. However, for consequences to mean anything, they have to occur when a student is not in an emotional state. The best practice is to de-escalate, then work on consequences. How to deal with consequences is discussed later in this chapter.

Anger is another common challenge. It does not have to be, however. Here's how to listen to an angry student:

Student (S): "He kicked me out of his class because he doesn't like me!"

You (Y): "You are angry."

S: "He called on me, I knew the answer, and he didn't like it 'cause he wanted me to look stupid!"

Y: "You feel disrespected."

S: "I told him that to his face because it's not right how he talks down at me, and he kicked me out! I don't care if he doesn't want me in his class—I don't want to be in his class either!"

Y: "You feel deeply insulted."

S: "He should be fired 'cause he's always doing stuff like that!"

Y: "You are angry."

S: "Yeah. How did you know that?"

Y: "You feel unloved and unwanted."

S: "Now my mom's gonna be pissed off at me."

Y: "You are afraid."

S: "But it's his fault because he was trying to make me look like a punk!"

Y: "You feel blamed for something that is not your fault."

S: "This sucks!"

Y: "You are really frustrated."

S: "Yeah!"

Remember, your immediate goal is to de-escalate the student and calm things down. You will find it a lot faster to affect label your students' emotions than to resist them, fight them, or threaten them. Once you have the head nod, you can move to problem-solving and consequences.

Dealing with Consequences

Our society holds a notion that justice equals punishment. The justifications for this notion include deterrence, punishment, power of authority over an individual, and vengeance, among others. There is little empirical data to support any of these justifications. Most punishment rationales have been developed as a way of explaining a visceral need to inflict pain on those who misbehave. Thus, schools have adopted zero-tolerance policies, aligning with the tough-on-crime advocates.

A paper by Brea L. Perry and Edward W. Morris, published in *American Sociological Review*, suggested that harsh discipline practices actually aren't good for anyone, including nonsuspended students. The researchers used data from the Kentucky School Discipline Study to examine whether and how out-of-school suspensions affect the academic achievement of nonsuspended students. They found: "High levels of out-of-school suspensions in a school over time are associated with declining academic achievement among non-suspended students, even after adjusting for a school's overall level of violence and disorganization."[18] In short, perfectly well-behaved students suffer from the effects of coercive social control, such as suspension and expulsion of misbehaving students.

Teachers do not want student misbehaviors to be tolerated. They rightfully desire calm and peaceful classrooms. They also feel a need to keep their authority and power over students as means of social and behavioral control. All of this is good. The question is how to do it effectively.

Effective school discipline requires a cooperative and coordinated effort by teachers, administrators, and parents. This is easier said than done because of time and resource restraints on all of the stakeholders. However, an effective, positive discipline system is fair, incremental, focuses on the core issues of the student, and uses discipline as a positive teaching moment. Properly designed and implemented restorative justice practices programs, such as Ron and Roxanne Claassen's Discipline That Restores©, have been shown to be very effective at positive school discipline. The foundation of any positive discipline system is the ability of an adult to affect label a student, then problem-solve to an agreement that makes things right and prevents future misbehavior.

Listening to Angry Parents

Every teacher has been confronted by angry parents. The encounters are never pleasant, and the teacher has the difficult task of remaining professional. Learning how to affect label an angry parent is a powerful tool that allows you, the teacher, to never become upset or angry. You can deal with the most insulting, threatening, and disrespectful parents effectively and move them into a place where a constructive conversation about their child can take place.

Your fundamental strategy in dealing with an angry or difficult parent is as follows:

1. Listen and affect label the parent's emotional experience in the moment.
2. When the parent calms down, core message what the parent is trying to communicate. (See chapter 5 on core messaging skills.)
3. Categorize the problem as within your control to address or not. Problems that you do not have control over include schoolwide policies, curriculum, and incidents and behaviors that occur outside your classroom. Parents with these issues should be referred to the administration.
4. Ask the parent for a solution. If the parent can offer up a solution, you are now in a negotiation. Some things can be negotiated; others cannot be. If the issue is a nonnegotiable one for you, offer a compromise on something that is negotiable. Everyone likes a deal. In this regard, you might think ahead and have a list of negotiables.
5. If you can fix the problem, do so and take responsibility for it.

6. If you can, seek an agreement that the parent will work on the problem at home. Make the deal mutual, with responsibilities on both sides.

7. Put it in writing. I know this sounds funny. However, simple agreements when in writing tend to be honored more often than verbal agreements.

8. Follow up in a few weeks to see how the parent is doing with the changes, if any.

Here are some scenarios that show how you might affect label an angry parent:

Parent (P): "I don't understand why you gave Deirdre a C-. She is a straight-A student. You must not be a very competent teacher."

You (Y): "You are frustrated and angry."

P: "Yes. How dare you give my A+ student such a low grade!"

Y: "You are afraid that Deirdre won't succeed."

P: "Yes. I know this is only third grade, but how will she get into medical school or law school?"

Y: "You are afraid that Deirdre won't be successful in life."

P: "Yes."

Y: "You are feeling unsupported in your parenting and don't think that anyone really cares."

P [crying]: Yes.

Y [pause to let the parent work through the emotions]: "Would you like to work on a plan to help Deirdre succeed academically?"

P: "Really? Yes. Please, what can I do?"

This conversation starts with a classic accusation and blaming statement directed at you. Most of the time, when a parent blames a teacher, the parent is feeling a complex set of emotions. Not being self-aware, the parent looks for the source of her emotional discomfort and tags you, the teacher, as the cause. Next time you sense blaming and accusation, recognize that, as disrespectful as it is, it is not about you.

You remain calm and affect label the surface emotions of anger and frustration. As you do that, the parent feels safe going further. As you simply reflect back her emotions, you gain the insight that Deirdre's mother is afraid. When you test that with an affect label, your guess is validated. Finally, you reach the core issues: fear and not being supported. Good job. The next move is to invite the mother into a problem-solving session in which she feels supported and in collaboration with you.

> **Parent (P):** "I think you are assigning too much homework. Raymond just does not have enough time after school to get it all done, and it is interfering with our family activities."
>
> **You (Y):** "You are frustrated and annoyed that Raymond has too much homework."
>
> **P:** "Yes. I mean, really, assigning four pages of math problems a night. Doesn't that seem too much for a seventh grader?"
>
> **Y:** "You are anxious."
>
> **P:** "Well, not anxious as much as concerned."
>
> **Y:** "You are concerned."
>
> **P:** "Yes. I am very concerned."
>
> **Y:** "Has Raymond complained to you?"
>
> **P:** "No."
>
> **Y:** "Hmmm. Well, he is doing excellent homework and is maintaining an A in the class. He is one of my top students."
>
> **P:** "I know. He is very proud of that. And that's the problem. He has to study all of the time and doesn't have time to be with me."
>
> **Y:** "You are feeling abandoned by Raymond."
>
> **P:** "Well, yeah. He is my best friend."
>
> **Y:** "So, you are feeling lonely."

P: "Yes."

Y: "How does Raymond feel about his homework?"

P: "He loves it. That's all he wants to do."

Y: "You are proud of his academic success."

P: "I really am!"

Y: "At the same time, you feel abandoned because he is putting his homework in front of spending time with you."

P: "Exactly."

The problem is not too much homework; it's the parent's loneliness and poor boundaries with Raymond. You are being blamed for the lack of connection when it seems like Raymond is using his homework as an excuse to be by himself and not be smothered. Instead of reacting defensively, you affect label through the problem until the inconsistency surfaces. Maybe the parent gets it or maybe not. However, you have provided a valuable service by reflecting these contradictory emotions in a way that allows the parent to process them. Usually, the parent will see the contradiction and begin to understand that the problem is with the parent, not you, the teacher.

Parent (P): "Jamie is just having too much difficulty with this Common Core curriculum. She is upset and frustrated that it is so hard."

You (Y): "You are worried that Jamie is struggling with the curriculum."

P: "Yes. She complains about it all of the time."

Y: "You are becoming weary of her complaining."

P: "I am. I know that the curriculum is more demanding, and I support that. But isn't there any easier way to transition into it?"

Y: "You are pleased with the rigor of the curriculum and are a little frustrated that there isn't an easier way into it."

P: "That's it."

Y: Would you mind telling me what kind of support you are giving to Jamie at home for her studies?"

P: "Well, we're mostly letting her struggle on her own."

Y: "Would you be open to some ideas about how to support her?"

P: "Sure."

How nice. This is a truly concerned parent who is invested in her child's success. Rather than become defensive or condescending about the curriculum, you take a few moments to validate her feelings with the affect labeling. Once you understand that this parent is truly concerned, you move into a problem-solving mode quickly. Remember the rules: de-escalate and then problem-solve.

Most people jump into problem-solving without understanding or validating the emotions. This almost always leads to feelings of not being heard and disrespect. Take a moment to pay attention to a parent's emotional experience. You will find that the problem-solving will proceed smoothly, and the parent will usually be grateful.

Here is a situation in which the parent is in denial about a lazy, unmotivated, unengaged child:

You (Y): "Thanks for coming in. I am concerned about Henry. His grades are poor. He seems completely unengaged and unmotivated to learn. I wanted to talk to you about that and see if we could come up with a plan to help him."

Parent (P): "Hey, my boy is doing just fine. He's star of the football team and is super popular. He's completely engaged in sports and school."

Y: "You are proud of Henry's sports achievements."

P: "You bet I am."

Y: "Well, how do you feel about his academic performance?"

P: "Hell, he's no Einstein. Besides, he's doing okay."

Y: "You are happy with his academic performance."

P [after a pause]: "Well, no, but he's not that bad."

Y: "You are a little anxious that he is not doing so well."

P: "Well…look, he's going to be fine."

Y: "You really are concerned about his academics and are confused about what to do about it."

P: "Well, yeah. I guess that's right."

Y: "You are a little frightened that he might fail in school, which would destroy any chance at a football career."

P: "Yeah, a little."

Y: "You and your wife would be really sad if Henry failed to reach his potential as a football player."

P: "Yeah. We would be disappointed."

Y: "You and your wife would be disappointed if Henry failed academically."

P [nodding]: "Yeah."

Y: "Okay, would you be willing to work on a plan to help him succeed?"

P: "Absolutely!"

This conversation is not so much about de-escalating strong emotions as it is helping a parent in denial who feels helpless to change his child's academic trajectory. You know that without buy-in from the parents, helping Henry will be tough, if not impossible. Getting to the root of the father's feelings is the first step in enlisting his aid.

At one point, you do a reverse affect label, without asking a question. This is a more advanced application of the skill. In reverse affect labeling, you label the opposite emotion of what you think is present. This is helpful when someone is in denial and cannot face the shame or embarrassment of the real emotion. Here's what happened:

Y: "Well, how do you feel about his academic performance?"

P: "Hell, he's no Einstein. Besides, he's doing okay."

Y: "You are happy with his academic performance."

P [after a pause]: "Well, no, but he's not that bad."

Y: "You are a little anxious that he is not doing so well."

P: "Well... look, he's going to be fine."

Y: "You really are concerned about his academics and are confused about what to do about it."

P: "Well, yeah. I guess that's right."

In this case, by saying, "You are happy with his academic performance," you help the father process his own concerns that he could not process on his own. Do not reverse affect label by asking, "Are you happy with his academic performance?" Asking a question activates a different response mechanism. The father knows he is not happy and has denied his concern. Asking him if he is happy may be interpreted as a judgment, a put-down, or a sarcastic comment. His reaction is bound to be defensive, and he is likely to escalate.

As counterintuitive as it seems, by reverse affect labeling you are not perceived as judging or criticizing. Affect labeling is a form of emotional granularization that helps people understand and process what they are actually feeling. A negative affect label forces a person to compare his or her emotional experience to the statement. People find it much easier to correct a negative affect label than to answer a question because answering a question, first, requires more cognitive processing power and, second, requires an uncomfortable level of vulnerability. I am continually amazed at how this slight shift between a statement and a question makes all the difference in helping people calm down.

Once Henry's father realizes that he is not happy, you continue to affect label him until he realizes how sad and disappointed he would be if Henry failed. At that point, problem-solving can begin.

Sometimes, parents are arrogant and annoyed to be wasting time in a teacher conference. Arrogance usually indicates a deeper insecurity, which comes from a deep need for attachment and an equally deep fear of rejection. Arrogance is the defense against the emotional pain of rejection.

You (Y): "Thanks for coming in to talk about your daughter's progress."

Parent (P): "This is a monumental waste of my time. Do you know how much I make per hour?"

Y: "You are angry and frustrated that you have to meet with me."

P: "I run an organization that is one of the largest employers in the region. Half of the parents of your students are employees of mine."

Y: "You feel disrespected and demeaned that you have to meet with me."

P: "I should be meeting with the chair of the school board about Brenda. I funded her election campaign."

Y: "You don't feel like you are receiving the respect you deserve."

P: "Absolutely right. Why should I have to deal with a teacher, of all people?"

Y: "You feel like talking with me is beneath you and insults your dignity."

P: "Yes, very true. Now, why am I here?"

Y: "Your daughter Brenda is having problems in math."

P: "That's her mother's responsibility, not mine."

Y: "You are frustrated that you have to deal with this issue."

P: "Of course. Wouldn't you be frustrated?"

Y: "You are frustrated and angry at Brenda's mother."

P: "Which is why we are divorced."

Y: "So, you are angry that you have to be here to deal with an issue you believe should be handled by Brenda's mother."

P [nodding]: "Yes, exactly."

Y: "Well, now that you are here, would you like to help come up with a plan to help Brenda succeed at math?"

P [sighing]: "I suppose."

Y: "You are resentful that you have to take on this task."

P: "I am an extremely busy and important man. Of course I am resentful."

Y: "How do you feel about Brenda failing math?"

P: "She's obviously not working hard enough. Probably because of her mother's neglect."

Y: "You are angry over your relationship with Brenda's mother."

P: "Very angry. And Brenda is suffering."

Y: "You are worried about Brenda."

P: "I am. I know she is not doing well in math. And I cannot convince her mother to help Brenda with homework."

Y: "You feel a little helpless over Brenda's homework."

P: "I do."

Y: "And you feel a little shame that you cannot be there for her."

P [quietly]: "Yes."

Y: "Would you be willing to talk about ways of supporting Brenda in her academics?"

P: "Of course I would."

Y: "Great."

This is a tough conversation. The father spews out one insult after another at you. He lacks self-awareness and is self-absorbed in his importance and influence. The normal response would be to dismiss him as an arrogant, disrespectful parent. In this case, you maintain your center and flow with his emotions. Finally, a crack opens, and you take a risk:

Y: "You are angry over your relationship with Brenda's mother."

P: "Very angry. And Brenda is suffering."

Y: "You are worried about Brenda."

P: "I am. I know she is not doing well in math. And I cannot convince her mother to help Brenda with homework."
Y: "You feel a little helpless over Brenda's homework."
P: "I do."
Y: "And you feel a little shame that you cannot be there for her."
P [quietly]: "Yes."

The father finally comes around to understanding his own shame and fear for his daughter. Although he blames Brenda's mother, he knows that he shoulders equal blame. Under normal circumstances, his low self-esteem would prevent him from acknowledging to himself that he is somewhat helpless and shamed. Part of the power of affect labeling is that it is nonjudgmental and noncritical. You are simply reflecting the emotional experience of the speaker. As you become an emotional mirror, the speaker—in this case, the father—can begin to process emotions that are too dangerous to otherwise deal with.

The most important lesson is to never react to the provocation. This man is deeply wounded. He has compensated by becoming financially successful, and his success has allowed him to become arrogant beyond belief. He probably has never experienced someone really listening to his emotions nonjudgmentally. The experience may be frightening. However, he does love his daughter and does feel helpless. He is really asking for help and does not know how to do so without seeming weak. Affect labeling is one way to throw out a life buoy.

Chapter Summary

In this chapter, we explored how teachers might use affect labeling to de-escalate students and parents. The takeaways are:

- Affect labeling is a powerful classroom management tool that de-escalates upset students and teaches emotional intelligence.
- Depending upon age and social and cognitive development, students have varying degrees of emotional categorization and granularization.
- Taking the time to understand the emotional lives of your students goes a long way toward managing their behaviors in your classroom.
- Validating a student's emotions is powerful.
- Remember to de-escalate first and then problem-solve.
- Coercive, punitive, zero-tolerance discipline systems do not have empirical evidentiary support. Restorative justice and practices systems have been shown to be superior at managing discipline, which means affect labeling.
- Affect labeling and core messaging are excellent tools when dealing with angry and upset parents. After de-escalating an emotionally upset parent, you can then look for ways to problem-solve together.

10

How to Be Civil in an Uncivil Society

In order for cooperation to get started in the first place, one more condition is required. The problem is that in a world of unconditional defection, a single individual who offers cooperation cannot prosper unless others are around who will reciprocate.

—**Robert Axelrod**, *The Evolution of Cooperation*

How do I have a relationship and continue to love someone who is oppositional and whose perspective I don't understand or respect? How can I be loved and respected despite my beliefs? How do I express myself in a way that does not offend, but speaks to my truth? How do I listen to others whose views I abhor? How can I foster cooperation and peace in my home and community?

The problems of a socially polarized world are plaguing our families and communities. Liberal family members can barely speak to conservative family members without one or the other or both ranting loudly. Facebook and Twitter seem to escalate everyone. No one is able to listen, understand, or converse civilly, especially when the topics are as personal and emotional as politics, religion, and culture. The situation is not helped by our high-level elected officials or leaders, who demonize each other, the media, and anyone who disagrees with them. What is going on here? And can we do anything about it?

The short answer is yes. Let's start with some science to help us understand the problem.

What Are Beliefs?

Beliefs are the conviction in the truth of some idea. Beliefs are different from other mind functions such as memory, knowledge, and attitude. We create beliefs, usually unconsciously, as a means of understanding the world we live in, and without beliefs to guide us, we would have to figure out the meaning of every new event or situation each time. Beliefs reserve our hard cognitive processing (for example, thinking) for truly unique challenges or problems.

Beliefs also provide a sense of community and security. Shared beliefs help define our groups. Beliefs allow us to create values around food, shelter, language, dress, behavior, religion, and morality. Beliefs also create shared meanings of the world between us. If you and I share a belief, we feel connected. We are able to cooperate more easily and communicate more clearly. If we hold different beliefs about something, we do not feel connected, find cooperation challenging, and may struggle to communicate.

Of course, beliefs vary in duration, intensity, and commitment. Duration suggests that some beliefs are long-lasting, while others are short-lived. One's belief in God is durable. One's belief that the Chicago White Sox will win the World Series may not be so durable. Beliefs may vary in intensity. We have strong beliefs, and we have weak beliefs. We protect what we intensely believe in and yield beliefs for which we have little investment. Beliefs also vary in commitment. Some beliefs can be easily changed; others so define us that changing them can be difficult.

Some beliefs are based on reasoning and logic. We believe that the Earth orbits the sun not because we have directly observed it but because we know that astronomers have performed the observations and calculations that establish the belief as true. Other beliefs are based on emotion. These beliefs make us feel good, soothe us, and create the appearance of a predictable world. Emotionally based beliefs are often created from an unconscious process known as *motivated reasoning*. Motivated reasoning is biased reasoning to produce emotionally preferable conclusions. In others words, our brain rationalizes or justifies a belief by ignoring contradictory facts or by making up facts that support the belief.

Generally, political polarization is caused by motivated reasoning. People engage in motivated reasoning to form political beliefs that are emotionally satisfying. In many cases, the underlying facts are ignored or skewed to fit a particular belief. And when faced with situations or facts that threaten the coherency of our beliefs, we attempt to resolve the inconsistency through the process of assimilation, which means that we change the facts to be consistent with the beliefs.

Motivated reasoning is, consequently, the process of making up facts or cherry-picking only favorable facts to support a belief rather than using all objective facts to reach a logical, but possibly unpleasant, conclusion. Instead of dealing with the emotionally painful and unfavorable empirical facts, an alternative story is claimed as the truth that fits and supports the person's belief. A belief created by motivated reasoning becomes stronger when confronted with conflicting, but truthful, information.

In one research study, participants were recruited for their political partisanship. Their brains were scanned while they were shown statements made by George W. Bush and John Kerry in the 2004 presidential campaign. Some of the candidate statements were consistent with the partisan beliefs. During those statements, the participants' brains were calm. However, when statements were presented that showed the partisan candidate to be untruthful, the emotional centers of the brain lit up. More significantly, many dopamine receptors became active. The partisan brain was rewarding itself for holding on to a strong belief in the face of true, but contradictory, facts. People just became more stubborn in their beliefs when faced with evidence that their beliefs were wrong.[19]

Listening to Polarized People

As I studied beliefs from the perspective of a mediator and peacemaker, I created four rules to help me resolve difficult disputes around ideologies and values. They are:

1. Never argue against an emotional belief, because logic and reasoning will not change an emotional mind.
2. Facts are not important, so ignore them.
3. Work toward understanding, not persuading.
4. Be patient, calm, sensitive, and compassionate.

The first rule, never argue against an emotional belief, is based on neuroscience. The studies show that arguing against an emotional belief strengthens, rather than weakens, the belief. We have all seen this with stubborn friends and relatives. They are not being stubborn just to be ornery. Their brains are flooding with dopamine to reinforce their beliefs. They have no conscious control of the process and cannot easily change a strong belief. You are wasting your time trying to change their minds.

The second rule is a hard one: the facts are not important, so ignore them. We all have a need to be right. Ignoring the facts seems like giving up on the truth. Well, there are times when this is the best strategy. Obviously, there are many situations where the truth must dictate outcomes. The scientific method is a rigorous application of hypothesis creation, experimentation, observation, and analysis designed to find the truth. One would never claim to ignore the facts in the pursuit of science, although history is full of examples where that happened. (Not so long ago, the conventional wisdom was that the world was flat and the sun rotated around the Earth. People were burned at the stake for claiming otherwise.) In dealing with polarized beliefs, we are not litigating a case in court. We do not need to win anything. What we are seeking is connection and relationship with someone who sees the world very differently.

The third rule follows from the first two: work toward understanding, not persuading. To work toward understanding means that we ask questions that will offer answers of deeper explanation. For example, here are seven questions I might ask someone who is politically polarized:

1. What life experiences led you to the values you hold today?

This is such a simple question, yet is so powerful. People do not reflect on what causes them to believe the way they do. Most beliefs are unconsciously formed. Until you ask about them, most people do not reflect upon their beliefs. When you ask how their values were formed, you are helping them understand themselves. Sometimes, you get a response like "I don't know." If the person you are talking with isn't prepared to do a little self-reflection, talk about the Super Bowl. You aren't going anywhere meaningful in that moment.

2. What is it about your values that make them important to you?

Values and beliefs create reality. Asking why values are important does not challenge them; it causes the other person to think about why they are important. Sometimes, this leads to circular thinking. Usually, others are grateful that you are making the inquiry.

3. How do you honor your values in everyday life?

This question can be discomfiting if the answer reveals inconsistency. For example, if your housekeeper is undocumented, and you support anti-immigration and deportation policies, there is a disconnection between values and behaviors. Many people will state strong beliefs, such as "I am totally against big government," yet not see the incongruity of also saying, "But don't mess with my Medicare or Social Security." When asking this question, you must not argue or try to prove a point. You have to come at this gently.

4. Do you ever work with people who have different values than you?

Most people don't think about whether people around them hold different values. People tend to believe that everyone is just like them and sees the world the same way. Asking this question causes some reflection on whether there are other beliefs out there.

5. How do you manage those relationships?

People mostly say that they try to avoid talking about beliefs that brew arguments. Again, this question causes reflection on the difference between actions and beliefs. A person might be perfectly fine with a Muslim neighbor but adamant about a strong vetting policy for Muslim immigrants. Asking a question like this can provide insight into how a polarized person really feels about politically hot issues.

6. When someone asserts belief in a value that is fundamentally different than your value, how do you feel?

Many people deny being upset by opposing values. We want to be seen as open, tolerant beings even though we may be grossly intolerant. Asking people what emotional experiences occur allows them to reflect on their emotional experience. You can follow up with a "Why?" question, such as "Why do you think you get upset when thinking about a woman's right to choose?"

7. How do you think a society composed of people with very different and opposing values should operate?

This question causes one to consider whether the polarization of society is the best way to coexist with differing values. You might run across a person who simply wants to be rid of anyone who is different. Well, at least you know what the feelings are all about. Change the subject to the weather.

The fourth rule to resolving difficult disputes around ideologies and values is to be patient, calm, sensitive, and compassionate. This is hard if you are deeply invested in a polar opposite belief. The easiest way to remain calm and sensitive is to rely on your powerful empathic listening skills. Respond to answers to your questions with core messaging and affect labeling, not with arguments, facts, and logic. Remember your goal: you want to understand and connect.

Here are some examples of how you might manage conversations with politically polarized people:

> **Samuel (S):** "I'm so pleased that our government is kicking out all of the illegal aliens in our country."
>
> **You (Y):** "You are happy about the government's immigration policy."
>
> **S:** "Damn straight I am."
>
> **Y:** "Tell me, Sam, what in your life brought you to the belief that illegal aliens should be kicked out?"
>
> **S:** "Heck, they steal our jobs and commit all kinds of crimes. Wouldn't you want them kicked out?"
>
> **Y:** "You are angry at illegal aliens allowed to steal jobs and commit crimes."
>
> **S:** "Yeah. What good are borders if there is no enforcement?"
>
> **Y:** "Having laws enforced is important to you."
>
> **S:** "Absolutely."
>
> **Y:** "And having people obey laws is important to you."
>
> **S:** "Yep. I am a law-and-order kind of guy."
>
> **Y:** "Knowing that laws are being obeyed and enforced makes you happy."
>
> **S:** "Sure does."
>
> **Y:** "You feel safer when everyone is following the same rules."
>
> **S:** "I never really thought of it that way, but you're right. I do feel safer when the rules are followed."

Y: "You like order and certainty in your life."

S: "I do."

Y: "So, kicking out illegal aliens makes you feel safe because law and order is being restored."

S: "You got it."

Y: "Yes, I think I do. Thanks, Sam, for helping me understand your feelings about this."

This conversation goes pretty well. Samuel starts off with a strong statement of belief. Your response is not to argue with him but to affect label his emotions. Samuel calms down immediately, so you try asking about how his belief was formed. As the conversation continues, you never challenge Samuel, never refer to facts, and always seek understanding.

You affect label Samuel's emotional experience and core message what you think are his underlying values. Obedience to lawful authority is important to Samuel because he craves security and certainty. Knowing that laws will be followed and enforced gives Samuel a sense of control. As he puts it, what good are borders if there is no enforcement? You will not change Samuel's mind about immigration policy. However, you have learned that Samuel has a need for an orderly, predictable universe, which is expressed in his belief that all illegal aliens should be deported.

Here's another contentious political topic, healthcare:

Irene (I): "I'm so pleased that our government is throwing out federally mandated health insurance."

You (Y): "You are happy about the end of federally mandated health insurance."

I: "I'm delighted. It was one of the worst laws ever passed."

Y: "What was the worst part of federally mandated health insurance in your view?"

I: "That if you didn't have insurance, you were fined by having to pay more taxes."

Y: "You were angry that the government was forcing people against their will to buy health insurance."

I: "Indeed. Health insurance is a private matter that the government should have no business regulating."

Y: "You strongly believe that government should stay out of people's lives."

I: "Absolutely."

Y: "And people should be allowed to fend for themselves for healthcare and health insurance."

I: "Yes. I strongly disagree with the idea that the government should be helping the poor purchase health insurance."

Y: "Hmmm. You dislike federally mandated health insurance because it takes away people's choices, restricting their freedom, and it benefits the poor at the expense of the wealthy."

I: "Yes. You summarized that very well."

Y: "Federally mandated health insurance represented a threat against freedom and a threat against the idea that everyone should take of themselves and not rely on the government."

I: "I never really thought of it that way, but you're right. I do feel that federally mandated health insurance threatened our freedom."

Y: "I'm curious about how your life experiences brought you to value freedom and individual responsibility."

I: "I was raised by parents who worked very hard and were financially successful. There came a time when the more money they made, the more they were taxed. They complained to us children bitterly. It's not fair to work hard and be successful only to have the government take away most of what you earned to give out welfare checks and food stamps."

Y: "To your way of seeing things, if you worked hard and earned money, fundamental fairness says that you shouldn't have to give up what you earned to someone who didn't work hard or earn anything."

I: "That's right. The welfare state is fundamentally unfair to those of us who were smart and hardworking enough to make money."

Y: "For you, the real issue is one of fairness."

I: "Yes, it is."

In this conversation, what could have been a blood-pressure-raising argument resulted in a deeper understanding of Irene's worldview. She sees things in the light of freedom and fairness. Knowing this, you can invite Irene into a problem-solving conversation about how to balance freedom and fairness as she sees it with the structural unfairness caused by racism, sexism, and poverty. Although you might not find agreement on policies, you could have a very instructive and civil conversation about the deeper problems in our society without challenging values.

These conversations take some skill and effort, but not a lot. Mostly, you have to be willing to listen and reflect rather than defend and attack. It's a different mindset than the combative attitudes that prevail.

Here's another situation, around the clash of religious and secular beliefs:

Josh (J): "I believe the liberalization of attitudes toward sexual orientation, transgender rights, and even abortion rights to be an abomination."

You (Y): "Tell me more."

J: "I feel like my faith and religion are being challenged and threatened every day by a culture that stands for that which I believe is evil and sinful."

Y: "You are angry and feel threatened."

J: "Everywhere around me, rules are changing. There is no such thing as moral behavior anymore."

Y: "You are frustrated and fearful."

J: "Yes. I feel like those of my faith are in a minority and our beliefs are dismissed. It's as if the teaching of Scripture is being swept away by a tidal wave."

Y: "You feel anxious that modern culture is sweeping away your beliefs."

J: "We are outnumbered. Despite the strength of our faith, we are being crushed. But we will not yield."

Y: "You no longer feel safe. The world is changing so fast, and there are so many attitudes that you abhor. You feel alone and isolated."

J: "Yes. Exactly. I don't even know how to understand these elites who dictate social morals to us."

Y: "You feel like your religious identity is being stripped from you."

J: "Yes, I do. It's very upsetting to be constantly confronted with people who are nonbelievers."

Y: "You are upset at having to be confronted with people who do not hold your beliefs."

J: "Yes. The bedrock of this country is the morality of Scripture. Now, all of that seems tossed aside."

Y: "You are fearful that if there are no moral guidelines, society will eventually collapse on itself."

J: "I hadn't thought about it that way, but yes, I think that's correct. God will punish us for leaving his path."

Y: "You feel a lot of anxiety around this."

J: "Yes, I do."

Y: "Thank you. I understand better what you have been experiencing."

J: "You are welcome, and thanks for listening to me."

Part of the polarization of society involves the stark contrast between religious and secular beliefs. People, regardless of their beliefs, experience anxiety when they perceive the encroachment of abhorrent beliefs into their lives. Arguing over whether a religious belief should dictate public policy or whether a secular idea should have precedence over religion is almost always counterproductive. The best we can hope for is understanding.

In the situation between Josh and you, you take the stance of listening. As Josh tries to explain his fears and anxieties, you affect label him. He is not about to convince you, and certainly there is no point in you trying to dissuade him. By listening deeply for understanding, you learn that Josh's great fear is loss of his identity. To him, the secular encroachment on his beliefs feels like an existential threat to his existence. Gaining that understanding and validating Josh's strong feelings builds a small bridge of trust. Someday, a deeper conversation about how to balance the rights of the some against the rights of others might be possible. For now, understanding is sufficient.

When Families Are Divided

Many families have been split apart over beliefs. Social media tends to aggravate the problem as friends and family feud online and in public spaces. Of course, Facebook is no place to have a meaningful conversation about anything. Yet Facebook and other online social networks have replaced many forms of communication between people.

While Facebook has allowed us to follow friends we might otherwise not be close to, it has also eliminated social space. Social media's immediacy demands instant response. Furthermore, we are no longer separated from one another by time or distance. It seems as if there is no longer any place to reflect and respond thoughtfully. There are no inherent social mechanisms for restraint or decorum. Unlike face-to-face conversations, there are no consequences to insults and disrespectful behavior. Reprimands mean nothing online. Further, none of the traditional ways of slowing down conversation work in social media. As a result, social media plays into our unconscious reactivity, triggers our beliefs without reflection, and accelerates polarization.

It should be no wonder that the communication habits formed from social media carry over to families (and any other personal relationships). Conversations between family members holding different beliefs may not be restrained, may lack decorum and respect, and may not be deliberative or sufficiently slow enough to allow for more thoughtful and meaningful exchanges. In short, families can become divided quickly. Once divided, the hurt feelings, isolation, sense of betrayal, lack of trust, disrespect, anger, and fear make reconciliation all the more difficult.

There is hope. As a mediator, I have seen thousands of conflicts, many of them between family members. In the vast majority of family disputes, reconciliation occurred. It can happen in your polarized family too. The work will be hard and perhaps painful, but the reward will be priceless.

In any polarized relationship, the first rule is: slow down.

What caused the division was reactivity, impulsivity, and irresponsibility. Restoring relationships requires restraint, respect, and personal accountability. You have to have mechanisms for slowing down your conversations to give everyone time to control their urge to speak first and loudest. Here are a couple of ways to do this:

Establish Some Conversational Ground Rules

The first technique is to simply agree on some conversational ground rules. I have found that people who cannot agree whether the sky is blue or the sky is black can agree on how they will behave when talking to each other. Usually, I describe the ground rules this way: "First, we agree that one person will speak at a time without interruption. We will probably hear things that we do not like, that will make us angry, that we think are lies, or that we otherwise think we need to respond to. Just take notes. Both of you will have an opportunity to speak when it is your turn. Can we agree to this ground rule?

"Second, when listening, we agree to summarize back both what the speaker has said and the feelings that the speaker has experienced. At first this will feel uncomfortable. Just because we are summarizing back does not mean, however, that we in any way agree with what the speaker said—it just shows everyone that we understand what they were trying to share with you. Can we agree to this ground rule?

"Third, we all agree that we will speak the truth from our hearts and our minds. Truth is very subjective, so what we are really trying to do here is speak to our personal experience as honestly as we can. We also want to speak about the facts and the feelings that come up around this conflict. Can we agree to this ground rule?

"Fourth, we agree to be respectful. That means that the words we choose, the tone of voice we use, and our body language will all be respectful even though we might be angry, upset, or annoyed in the moment. Can we agree to this ground rule?

"Finally, this mediation has to be fair. We each have the right to question anything that does not seem right or fair. Can we agree to this ground rule?"

To summarize the ground rules:

1. One person speaks at a time without interruption.
2. The listener agrees to summarize and reflect back emotions and feelings.
3. We agree to speak our truth.
4. We agree to be respectful with words, tone of voice, and body language.
5. We agree to be fair.

I have found that agreeing to these simple ground rules creates a sense of order and safety that allows for more difficult conversations to take place. When listening and reflecting is required, it imposes concentration on the listener to pay attention. The actual reflection slows the conversation down, giving everyone time to think about what is being said and assuring some understanding.

Of course, the ground rules are frequently violated despite the best of intentions. The most effective way to deal with a violation is to ask a recommitment question. Suppose John gets sarcastic when talking. You might respond with: "John, what is your commitment to ground rule number four, being respectful?"

Telling John he was disrespectful will bring a heated denial. The better strategy is to find out where John is in his original commitment. By asking him a question, John has to stop, think, and respond. The question slows him down enough to let him compare his behavior to his commitment. Almost always, that is enough. If you are able, you can affect label John's response to your question:

> **You (Y):** "John, what's your commitment to being respectful?"
> **John (J):** "Uh. Oh, I guess I was getting angry and sarcastic."
> **Y:** "You were angry as you were talking and became sarcastic."
> **J:** "Yeah, exactly. I'm sorry. I am committed to being respectful. Thanks for calling it out."

Most people most of the time want their actions to be consistent with their commitments. By asking about John's commitment, you are gently asking him about his desire to be consistent with what he agreed to. It is not challenging because John can always retract his commitment. If he does so, the conversation will be suspended for another time. If he reaffirms his commitment to be respectful, he will probably try very hard to be so.

When listening, use paraphrasing, affect labeling, and core messaging in your reflection as appropriate. Do not expect an untrained listener to reflect very well back to you. You might coach a little to help out. However, you have to be satisfied with whatever your listener can come up with. Applying ground rules to a conversation with a polarized family member is a simple way to rebuild trust and common ground.

Using Peace Circles to Slow Down

I introduced peace circles in chapter 4. A peace circle is essentially a time and place for telling stories. Unlike many other conversations, participants in peace circles are mostly silent as they listen to the stories of others. The peace circle experience is not like a normal conversation, because of its structure; it allows for deeper, richer communication and time to reflect.

If you have five or more family members who have been affected by polarization, for example, convening them in a peace circle is a powerful and safe way to talk about deep-seated differences.

When convening a circle to talk about a tough subject, think carefully about the ritual. The centerpiece should be something aesthetic and calming. Flowers or a large candle are great centerpieces. Likewise, the talking piece should be something symbolic. If the circle will take up a heavy topic, maybe a large bird feather would be appropriate. The lightness of the feather symbolically contrasts with the density of what is to be talked about.

The circle keeper establishes ground rules, for instance, using the five we just discussed, so that everyone agrees to the same conduct. Then the circle keeper poses questions around the topic that cause reflection and sharing. For example, using one of the seven questions I draw from when talking with someone who is politically polarized, the circle keeper might start a circle by asking, "What life events brought you to the beliefs that you have today around immigration?"

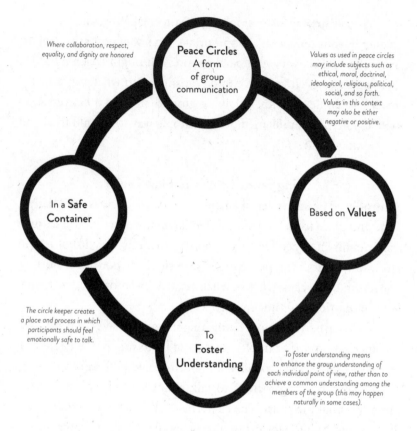

Where collaboration, respect, equality, and dignity are honored

Peace Circles A form of group communication

Values as used in peace circles may include subjects such as ethical, moral, doctrinal, ideological, religious, political, social, and so forth. Values in this context may also be either negative or positive.

In a **Safe** Container

Based on **Values**

The circle keeper creates a place and process in which participants should feel emotionally safe to talk.

To **Foster Understanding**

To foster understanding means to enhance the group understanding of each individual point of view, rather than to achieve a common understanding among the members of the group (this may happen naturally in some cases).

Remember to move clockwise, so the person to the circle keeper's left is the first to answer. The circle keeper hands her the talking piece, signifying her right to speak. When she is done, she hands the talking piece to the person on her left, who paraphrases, core messages, and affect labels what she said. The two exchange the talking piece until the speaker is satisfied that the listener accurately reflected what was said. The listener becomes the new speaker, and the process repeats.

Because circles slow the conversational process to a crawl, everyone has time to reflect and adjust to what is being said. Each person should speak for ninety seconds or so. That is a surprisingly long time when one is being reflective rather than reactive. No one is ever forced to talk and may pass when the talking piece comes around. However, passing on speaking does not mean passing on listening and reflecting. Everyone has to listen and reflect the person to the right.

Here are some questions that work when polarized families sit in a circle:

- What three values are most important to you?
- How do those values express themselves in your life?
- How will you live by those values in the next week?

Here's another set of typical questions:

- What is hope?
- How is hope expressed in your life?
- What will you do to create hope in the next week?

The peace circle formula is easy: the first part is to ask broad and open questions, such as the meaning of value and hope; then the second part is to ask reflection questions, turning to the speaker's life; the third is a call to action. The questions form around values such as hope, respect, love, charity, tolerance, open-mindedness, kindness, and so forth. Asking and speaking to these values reminds everyone in the circle that they have more shared values and beliefs than differences. The humanity and essential love of the family is allowed to pierce the bitterness of polarization.

We have taught this process to prison inmates as a stepping-stone to mediation. Our students are usually skeptical until they try it out. When they report back on their experiences with the first circles, they are uniformly amazed and enthusiastic adopters of the process.

Chapter Summary

In this chapter, we confronted and developed strategies to deal with polarized people and family members. We learned:

- About the nature of beliefs
- Why people engage in motivated reasoning
- How to listen to polarized people
- How online social networks accelerate polarization
- The importance of slowing down the conversation and finding understanding
- How to use ground rules to create a safe conversation
- How to convene people in a peace circle to share common ground

Afterword

In today's polarized and uncivil society, we can no longer treat peace as a noun; it is a verb. Each of us has the responsibility to create the peace we want around us. Peace is not kumbayah or touchy-feely. As I tell the inmates, becoming a peacemaker is one of the hardest callings a person can seek.

Conflict involves strong emotions, nasty words, disrespectful behaviors, and sometimes violence. The peacemaker steps into this morass with two goals: to de-escalate and to help people solve problems. The process is not linear, not predictable, and not always very much fun. It is, however, an essential skill for the twenty-first century and beyond. As Gandhi was reputed to have said, "If we continue with an eye for an eye and a tooth for a tooth, we will soon live in a blind, toothless world."[20] As many of our elected and public officials demonstrate incivility and the inability to solve difficult problems without conflict, we have to take it upon ourselves to be role models and teachers for those around us.

Knowing that we are each responsible for peace is not enough. The skills of peace are counterintuitive and require mastery that comes only from practice. We have to fight against our programmed reactivity, our tendency to stereotype, and our tendency to morally disengage. Since these are biases and heuristics that seem to be hardwired into us and operate outside of consciousness, they are hard to recognize in operation and harder still to counter.

So far, the only peacemaking skills I have learned that are consistently effective are those I have taught in this book. I am hopeful that as our knowledge of the human brain and mind increases, more insights will lead to more skills. For the time being, these de-escalating skills are foundational to training any person how to respond to strong emotions in a positive, validating way without losing composure or control.

Of course, reading a book is not a substitute for practice. And, as with any new skill, practicing means making mistakes. There will be times when you clumsily affect label. You will get pushback. The pushback doesn't mean the skill doesn't work; it means that you were not subtle enough or did not choose the right moment. Take it as a small lesson and not as an indication that affect labeling does not work. With practice over a few short weeks, you will find yourself naturally listening to emotions and affect labeling. When it becomes habitual, you will begin to see startling reactions from people around you. Arguments will defuse quickly, and you will become deeply appreciated by another person as someone "who finally gets me."

I hope that this book is widely read, and the practices and skills I teach become commonplace in our families, schools, communities, and institutions. I hope that organizational leaders learn how to use these skills to be more effective. I hope that parents stop invalidating their children's emotions, instead reflecting those emotions back. I hope that teachers learn how to engage their students more deeply by reading the emotional data fields in the classroom and responding appropriately. If even 1 or 2 percent of the population practiced these skills regularly, I think we would see a very different culture.

I am always interested in stories. Please contact me through my website, www.dougnoll.com, if you have a good one. Now, go and make peace.

Acknowledgments

I would like to acknowledge my colleague and cofounder of Prison of Peace, Laurel Kaufer. You are a force of nature, Laurel. Without your indomitable spirit, we would have never succeeded on our amazing journey together. I would also like to thank my friend and literary agent, Devra Jacobs, who has walked me through the book process three times now. To Rebecca Stinson, my publicist, you are a genius. To my dear friend, jazz violin teacher, and fellow author Julie Lyonn Lieberman, our biweekly lessons have always been far more than just music. Thank you. Finally, to my wife, Aleya Dao, your brilliance outshines the rest of us combined.

Notes

1. Robert Axelrod, *The Evolution of Cooperation* (New York: Basic Books, Inc., 1984), 63.

2. Douglas E. Noll, *Peacemaking: Practicing at the Intersection of Law and Human Conflict* (Telford, PA: Cascadia Publishing House, 2003), 150–85.

3. "Phaedrus by Plato," accessed February 25, 2017, http://classics.mit.edu/Plato/phaedrus.html.

4. "Discourse on the Method of Rightly Constructing One's Reason and Seeking Truth in the Sciences by René Descartes (1637)," accessed February 25, 2017, http://www.earlymoderntexts.com/assets/pdfs/descartes1637.pdf.

5. Rikki Lund, Ulla Christensen, Charlotte Juul Nilsson, Margit Kriegbaum, and Naja Hulvej Rod, "Stressful Social Relations and Mortality: A Prospective Cohort Study," *Journal of Epidemiology & Community Health*, 68 (2014): 720–27, http://dx.doi.org/10.1136/jech-2013-203675.

6. Hans-Rüdiger Pfister and Gisela Böhm, "The Multiplicity of Emotions: A Framework of Emotional Functions in Decision Making," *Judgment and Decision Making*, 3, no. 1 (2008): 5–17.

7. "A Primer of Affect Psychology by Vernon C. Kelly, Jr. (2009)," accessed March 19, 2017, http://www.tomkins.org/wp-content/uploads/2014/07/Primer_of_Affect_Psychology-Kelly.pdf.

8. Debra Umberson, Kristi William, and Kristin Anderson, "Violent Behavior: A Measure of Emotional Upset?" *Journal of Health and Social Behavior*, 43 (June 2002): 189–206.

9. Vincent J. Felitti, Robert F. Anda, Dale Nordenberg, David F. Williamson, Alison M. Spitz, Valeria Edwards, Mary P. Koss, James S. Marks, "Relationship of Childhood Abuse and Household Dysfunction to Many of the Leading Causes of Death in Adults: The Adverse Childhood Experiences (ACE) Study," *American Journal of Preventive Medicine* 14, no. 4 (1998): 245–58.

10. I would like to acknowledge the work of Ridge Associates and Robert Bolton, PhD. His early work was a foundation for my work and the Prison of Peace curriculum. Robert Bolton, *People Skills: How to Assert Yourself, Listen to Others, and Resolve Conflicts* (New York: Simon & Schuster, 1979).

11. Sidney Zisook and Katherine Shear, "Grief and Bereavement: What Psychiatrists Need to Know," *World Psychiatry* 8, no. 2 (2009): 67–74.

12. Lorne Campbell and Tara Marshall, "Anxious Attachment and Relationship Processes: An Interactionist Perspective," *Journal of Personality* 79, no. 6 (2011): 917–47 doi:10.1111/j.1467-6494.2011.00723.x; Tianyuan Li and Darius K. S. Chan, "How Anxious and Avoidant Attachment Affect Romantic Relationship Quality Differently: A Meta Analytic Review," *European Journal of Social Psychology* 42, no. 4 (2012): 406–19.

13. Matthew D. Lieberman, Naomi I. Eisenberger, Molly J. Crockett, Sabrina M. Tom, Jennifer H. Pfeifer, and Baldwin M. Way, "Putting Feelings into Words: Affect Labeling Disrupts Amygdala Activity in Response to Affective Stimuli," *Psychological Science* 18, no. 5 (2007): 421–28.

14. Ms. Humiston was released from prison on parole after more than twenty years of incarceration. Today, she is happily married with children and leading an exemplary life as a model citizen.

15. Kristen A. Lindquist and Lisa Feldman Barrett, "Emotional Complexity," in M. Lewis, J. M. Haviland-Jones, and L. F. Barrett (Eds.), *The Handbook of Emotions*, 3rd Edition (New York: Guilford, 2010).

16. Eckhart Tolle, *The Power of Now: A Guide to Spiritual Enlightenment* (Novato, CA: New World Library, 1999), 29.

17. STOIC is the core of the evidence-based CHAMPS approach to classroom behavior management. For a review of the empirical studies, see http://www.safeandcivilschools.com/research/references/is-champs-evidence-based.pdf.

18. Brea L. Perry and Edward W. Morris, "Suspending Progress: Collateral Consequences of Exclusionary Punishment in Public Schools," *American Sociological Review* 79, no. 6 (2014): 1067–87.

19. Drew Westen, Pavel S. Blagov, Keith Harenski, Clint Kilts, and Stephan Hamann, "Neural Bases of Motivated Reasoning: An fMRI Study of Emotional Constraints on Partisan Political Judgment in the 2004 U.S. Presidential Election," *Journal of Cognitive Neuroscience* 18, no. 11 (2006): 1947–58.

20. The phrase was used by Gandhi's biographer Louis Fischer to describe Gandhi's satyagraha philosophy. See Garson O'Toole, *The Quote Investigator*, accessed March 8, 2017, http://quoteinvestigator.com/2010/12/27/eye-for-eye-blind/.

Additional Resources

If you are interested in learning more about the skills and techniques I present in this book, here are some resources:

1. It's Pure Magic Online Course. This eight-video series teaches you the essential skills of affect labeling through online explanations, demonstrations, and exercises for you to practice. For more information, visit: http://itspuremagic.com.
2. The Doug Noll YouTube channel. You will find many of my lectures, presentations, and training sessions on my YouTube channel: http://bit.ly/2rHPkYx.
3. For more information about my workshops, advanced training, and keynote speaking, visit my website: http://dougnoll.com.
4. For more information about Prison of Peace, visit: http://prison ofpeace.org.

About the Author

Douglas E. Noll, JD, MA, is a full-time peacemaker and mediator, specializing in difficult, complex, and intractable conflicts. He has a masters degree in peacemaking and conflict studies. Noll was a business and commercial trial lawyer for twenty-two years before turning to peacemaking. He is a fellow of the International Academy of Mediators, on the American Arbitration Association panel of mediators and arbitrators, and one of the first United States mediators certified under the international mediator standards established by the International Mediation Institute.

Noll is the creator of Negotiating Mastery for the Legal Pro, an online negotiating training course, and Negotiate a Centered Life, an online life skills and relationship course. He is the author of *Elusive Peace: How Modern Diplomatic Strategies Could Better Resolve World Conflicts*; *Sex, Politics & Religion at the Office: The New Competitive Advantage* with John F. Boogaert; and *Peacemaking: Practicing at the Intersection of Law and Human Conflict*, as well as numerous articles about peacemaking, restorative justice, conflict resolution, and mediation.

His many accolades include recognition as a Northern California Super Lawyer, listed on the 2005 "Best Lawyers in America" by *US News & World Report*, 2012 *California* magazine California Attorney of the Year in conjunction with his colleague Laurel Kaufer for the Prison of Peace project, Encore Fellow 2014 by encore.org for his prison work, 2014 Lawyer of the Year by the Best Lawyers in

America website, and the Who's Who of International Commercial Mediators.

Noll is an adjunct professor of law at San Joaquin College of Law, a core faculty member of the American Institute of Mediation, adjunct faculty member of the Pepperdine School of Law's Straus Institute, and faculty member of the Straus Institute's Professional Skills Program. He serves as a speaker, teacher, lecturer, and workshop presenter nationally and internationally. Visit his website at dougnoll.com.